The Leadership Identity Journey

The Leadership Identity Journey

An Artful Reflection

Carol A. Mullen, Fenwick W. English,
and William A. Kealy

ROWMAN & LITTLEFIELD
Lanham • Boulder • New York • Toronto • Plymouth, UK

Published by Rowman & Littlefield
4501 Forbes Boulevard, Suite 200, Lanham, Maryland 20706
www.rowman.com

10 Thornbury Road, Plymouth PL6 7PP, United Kingdom

British Library Cataloguing in Publication Information Available

Library of Congress Cataloging-in-Publication Data

Mullen, Carol A.
The leadership identity journey : an artful reflection / Carol A. Mullen, Fenwick W. English, and William A. Kealy.
p. cm.
Includes bibliographical references and index.
ISBN 978-1-4758-0857-5 (cloth : alk. paper) -- ISBN 978-1-4758-0858-2 (pbk. : alk. paper) -- ISBN 978-1-4758-0859-9 (electronic)
1. Educational leadership. 2. Educational leadership--Philosophy. I. English, Fenwick W. II. Kealy, William A. III. Title.
LB2805.M775 2014
371.2'011--dc23

2014009631

♾™ The paper used in this publication meets the minimum requirements of American National Standard for Information Sciences Permanence of Paper for Printed Library Materials, ANSI/NISO Z39.48-1992.

Printed in the United States of America
Original cover art designed by William A. Kealy

To Brian Shabanowitz, the Wizard of Oz behind the scenes, for his encouraging colleagueship, team spirit, and fiscal magic.

For Fenwick English's father Melvin English who taught him the art of photography and how to make good prints in the darkroom.

In loving memory of Raymond W. Kulhavy, a great educational psychologist, leader, and friend.

Contents

List of Figures

List of Tables

Acknowledgments

Rowman & Littlefield Education's publishing team supported this project and assisted in the publication of our work. We are grateful to Dr. Thomas Koerner, vice president and publisher, who believed in the merit of our ideas and shepherded this project. Carlie Wall, assistant editor, provided timely communications.

All three coauthors worked collaboratively on figures 1.1, 2.1, 2.2, 2.3, and 4.1. William Kealy created the original work reflected in figure 5.1.

With respect to permissions, SAGE Publications provided permission to reprint figure 1.1 from F. W. English (2008b), *The Art of Educational Leadership: Balancing Performance and Accountability* (Thousand Oaks, CA: SAGE Publications).

Rowman & Littlefield Education gave permission to reprint figure 2.3, the original source of which is as follows: F. W. English (2008a), *Anatomy of Professional Practice: Promising Research Perspectives on Educational Leadership* (Lanham, MD: Rowman & Littlefield Education).

Figure 3.1 is commissioned by the Department of Agriculture (*Wikipedia*), Library of Congress, Prints & Photographs Division, FSA/OWI Collection, LC-USF34-9058-C. Copyright information specific to this photograph is at this Library of Congress website: http://search.loc.gov:8765/cs.html?charset=utf8&url=http%3A//www.loc.gov/rr/print/list/128_migm.html&qt=url%3A/rr/print/+%7C%7C+migrant+mother&col=loc&n=1&la=en.

Dorothea Large photographed for the U.S. Farm Security Administration/Office of War Information (FSA-OWI). The copyright and attribution information for work performed for this agency is at this Library of Congress website: www.loc.gov/rr/print/res/071_fsab.html.

Foreword

Confessions of a (Reforming) Structural-Functionalist

The foreword sections of most scholarly books focus on the way the volume contributes to the field of study. I have written forewords like this and while enjoyable it is not particularly taxing. This foreword, in contrast, is written so that anyone who reads it will understand the impact the work underlying this book has had on me—and its potential for doing the same for others. This is a personal statement as well as an endorsement of the line of work opened up by Mullen, English, and Kealy, and its significance for the development of educational leaders.

THE EMERGENCE OF EDPA 8020: A TOE IN REFLECTIVE WATERS

More than a decade ago, my colleagues observed that the name of our department was Educational Policy and Administration, and that we touted our programs for future leaders and scholars in higher education, preK–12 settings, and international development. We had, however, no doctoral course that covered leadership. I was asked to develop such a course, which was called Leadership: From Theory to Reflective Practice (EdPA 8020).

As I began to look for the best recent research on leadership that could provide a basis for that course, I was dismayed. Much of it focused on specific roles (e.g., principals, university presidents), which meant that it would not appeal to the wide variety of future scholars and scholar-practitioners served by our department and college. A great deal of the research outside of the field I knew best (K–12 leadership) was methodologically weak, and even more seemed to focus on either sweeping generalizations or specific administrative behaviors.

The most highly cited management authors seemed to be writing for the one-minute manager "airport leadership" crowd—people who pick up a book for light reading on the way from one important meeting to another. So much of the writing, even by well-regarded scholars, was a mad dash for leadership-by-adjective: putting a new descriptive word in front of *leadership* (shared leadership, strategic leadership, transformational leadership, charismatic leadership, servant leadership, and ethical leadership) might help to assure a place on the bestseller shelf.

As I battled my way back from the search engine rabbit holes of JSTOR and Business Source Premier, I reconsidered the question at the heart of designing any new learning experience: What was the purpose of having students spend time (and money) reading and discussing any selection of contemporary studies that I could find?

I settled on the goal of using seminal studies or materials that would serve two objectives. The first (more traditionally academic) was to ask students to grapple with the evolution of thinking about leadership, beginning with classic writers like Sun Tzu and Plato, and moving through contemporary theorists like Margaret Wheatley. Along the way (once we reached the mid-twentieth century and the rise of empiricism), I added in classic empirical studies that also contributed to theorizing about leadership, ranging from Ronald Lippett (1939) to Karl Weick (1993). But the overarching goal of a historical meandering through the thicket of leadership studies was to allow students—most of whom had worked in leadership positions—to reflect on their own experiences and to develop their own personal integrated theory-in-practice. In other words, I hoped to stimulate cognitive-rational and intuitive-perceptive opportunities.

After trolling among my colleagues at the University Council for Educational Administration (UCEA), I came across Bob Kottkamp and Karen Osterman's work on reflective practice at Hofstra, and they mentioned that they used movies to stimulate discussion about leadership work.[1] Bob pointed me in the direction of the Hartwick Humanities in Management Institute's leadership case series, which focuses on movies and literature as professional-development opportunities for leaders in all fields.[2] I was intrigued, and immediately incorporated some of these materials into my emerging course, which I taught (with some success) to three cohorts of students starting in the early 2000s. In order to encourage group and individual reflection, I chose to teach the course in six-hour blocks, reasoning that it was too easy for students who came to an executive evening program to "zone out" when reflection was demanded after a hard day at work. But something was still missing.

WE ARE WHAT WE EXPERIENCE

The moment of confession: I am personally more comfortable in the world of abstract empiricism than that of emotion and intuition. I had been a "get it done" kind of leader who is better at initiating new programs, completing tasks, and mediating temporary conflicts than in attending to individual needs and group dynamics.

In this regard, I am a product of my time. I came of age, intellectually, in the mid-1960s, when strategic protest, changing structures, and an immersion in the *New York Review of Books* were the *sine qua non* of the leftish academic who wanted to remake organizations (and therefore society). I had graduated from college and had my head down acquiring survey research skills when the "summer of love" and its affirmation of sensory awareness came along. I hurtled through my early leadership positions in a private research setting by adopting the organization's focus on "more, better, faster, cheaper"—a joke, but also somewhat accurate. Speed, accuracy, and meeting funder's needs were valued over reflection, since the organization's goal was growth.

The difficulty that I had developing a course syllabus and the self-doubts that attended teaching in a very different way suggested that I was the one who needed this course more than the students who were enrolling.

FINDING AN EMOTIONAL CENTER, AN INITIAL DEAD-END

In the mid-1990s, the idea of emotional intelligence (first coined by Yale psychologist Peter Salovey and the University of New Hampshire's John Mayer earlier in that decade) burst onto the leadership scene. Daniel Goleman's (1996) book on the topic became a bestseller, and spent more than a year and a half on the *New York Times* bestseller list. I never read it, and dismissed the idea as just another effort to popularize the obvious.

Not surprisingly, as a perusal of *Phi Delta Kappan*, *Ed Leadership*, and *Change*[3] in the late 1990s will attest, educators were among the first to pick up on the leadership implications of balancing an emphasis on student achievement in STEM with more attention to socioemotional development and attendant arts and humanities subjects. However, the general management research journals also began to articulate the intersection between emotional intelligence and effective leadership. A special issue of the *Journal of Organizational Behavior* was devoted to emotions in 2000; by 2005, one of the most prestigious journals in the field published an article that put cognitive intelligence head-to-head with emotional intelligence as a predictor of job performance (and found them to be compensatory using some outcome measures).

While many academics viewed the introduction of a-rational elements into the leadership literature as a potential antidote to the rising testing and accountability movement, others were more cautious. As one observer pointed out, tying emotional intelligence to leadership represented the "instrumentalization of the expressive, or the rationalization of the emotions for performative purpose" (Hartley, 1999, p. 309). In the general management theory, emotional intelligence was sometimes stripped of its potential and became synonymous with the banal concept of "social skills" (Barron & Gideon, 2000), or with the capacity to "manage emotions."

To a nonbeliever, the rapid adaptation by management gurus of the fundamental assumptions underlying the psychological research on emotional intelligence confirmed the nascent suspicion that leadership studies were all-too-often an instrument for manipulation rather than liberation. Clinging to my coming-of-age roots in the early to mid-1960s, I continued to focus on integrating leadership classics with humanities. The reflection that I asked of my students (and me) was largely analytic and intellectual—developing a personal theory of leadership that could be tied to seminal theories and empirical work, as reflected in literature and film. Feelings were addressed, but lightly and in passing.

A NEW PATH FOR THE LEADERSHIP JOURNEY

In 2009, at the UCEA meetings in Anaheim, I wandered into a session where Fenwick English and Carol Mullen presented a paper with the unexciting title "Exploring the Career Trajectories of Educational Practitioners." As usual, the presentations were all too brief, but I was intrigued with the way in which they were using Joseph Campbell's idea of the hero's journey to encourage educational leaders to reflect deeply on their career experiences.

Campbell's work is well known, but what struck me as inspirational, as I followed up with some superficial reading after the conference, was that he used his own theories about life as a journey to understand his life experiences and work: It was not just a synthesis of myth, but a structured way to explore modern "man." Mullen and English grabbed that idea and ran with it.

I almost immediately wrote to Fenwick and Carol and asked them for the full paper. I almost as quickly asked them to tell me more about the research process that they used, which involved presenting their participants with photographs and asking them to choose among them in response to different questions. My first response was that if movies, novels, and biographies could serve as a stimulus to integrate the personal and the analytic, why not photographs? I asked their permission to use the method in a different way—not to conduct research on leadership life courses, but as a strategy to help my students in the integration process that I was hoping for. They graciously responded and sent me the files that they used, asking only that I provide them with feedback about how it went.

I altered the approach that they took in their paper when I introduced the hero's journey-plus-photographs as a final integrative experience in EdPA 8020 in spring 2010. Rather than working with participants on individual responses, I pasted the photographs in the groups that Carol and Fenwick suggested onto large wall hangings so that multiple people could look at them at once. I had the class (which by then was more like a team of learners) look at the photographs, using the same five question probes that the authors had used in their research. (The prompts are discussed in detail in chapter 2.) Students were asked to record their responses on a prepared grid, and to explain the reason for their choices in smaller groups, where they could discuss how the pictures affected them and how they reflected underlying assumptions that were drawn from both leadership readings and their life experiences.

The responses were overwhelmingly positive, and many of the comments they made paralleled those that are reported in this volume. My students also placed a high value on using the pictures as a way of summarizing where they started out on their leadership journey, and where their choices indicated they might be headed. Since the final course paper asked them to integrate across both course readings/movies/other stimuli and their emerging personal leadership theories, the activity (which took about three hours) was seen as a valuable advance organizer. As a result, I began to look again at the writing on emotions in the workplace, and even to the idea of emotional intelligence. While not exactly a convert, I could see that in teaching an appeal to the emotional side of learning was as important as the specific articles that I assigned.

I excitedly emailed English and Mullen in May 2010, letting them know that the method was applicable not only to research with individual experienced leaders, but also to professional development with a group of people who were somewhat younger in the career stage. They indicated that I could continue to use the method as long as we stayed in touch; I, in turn, began to badger them to write a book that would put the method and the underlying assumptions into the hands of a larger audience. Four years later the book has transpired and we are about to begin a new journey.

FULL IMMERSION: AN ONGOING EPILOGUE

In spring 2012 I was invited to be the final presenter at a residential conference for women educational leaders. I agreed, but my heart sank when I realized that I was not being asked to present my research but rather to engage with the conference theme "Telling Our Stories." I am not fazed at the thought of giving a one-hour lecture to several hundred people; the challenge of wrapping up a small conference where the previous presenters were well-known on the women's leadership circuit left me a bit anxious. I then realized that Carol and Fenwick had put the tools in my hands. I returned to Campbell, and revised the hero's journey to align with Maddock's (1990) feminist perspectives.

Once that work was completed, the application of the photographs and the critical questions was simple and proved moving, particularly since the use of the feminist model allowed the group of professionals to talk in depth. They opened up about the darkness they sometimes faced as they negotiated space for influence while holding on to their attachment to the safe "home" of traditional feminine roles. With a group composed only of women who knew each other, comments about the personal and emotional meaning of the photographs they had chosen were sometimes quite different than those that I had encountered with a mixed-gender group of students. I had only two hours with the conference group: While we could have used more, the activity worked.

This experience leads me to two conclusions. The first is that the research potential of the original materials presented in this book must be explored further. For example, one persistent issue that I noticed at the summer conference was the strong desire on the part of some female professionals to avoid the feminist version of the journey in favor of the traditional Campbell version, while others immediately saw themselves in Maddock's revision. The immediate question of course is why. And would those differences be as apparent in individual interviews (such as those reported in this book)? Is there reason to consider other modifications to the basic work by Campbell that would better reflect the unique experiences of other previously marginalized groups entering leadership positions?

A second conclusion is that the potential for the approach that Mullen, English, and Kealy describe could significantly enhance team-building and development in groups where more knowledge of each other's noncognitive skills may enhance the capacity to be creative and open (Druskat & Wolff, 2001). The energy I've felt when using the materials in groups that have some familiarity with each other is palpable, but they have been "temporary organizations" where participants will leave at the end of the session (e.g., class, semester, conference) and have little need to rely on each other in the future.

Not surprisingly, a few consulting organizations have already launched programs that promise to increase the emotional intelligence of a group. I suspect that the approach presented in this book could be used to build a group level of emotional intelligence more quickly and possibly in a shorter period of time than other sensitivity training.

I could say more about my personal conversion process (ongoing) and my gratefulness to the authors of this book for their generous inclusion of me as a co-conspirator. However, I am mostly pleased that they have completed this publication so that others can experience and make use of their ideas. The main message that I hoped to convey is that when people see and write about their leadership experience as a journey, it is more than a moving experience: it can increase emotional intelligence and therefore enhance their personal and professional capacity. This book is based on research but is very practical. It can and should be used as well as admired.

Karen Seashore Louis, PhD,[4]
Regents Professor and Robert H. Beck Chair,
University of Minnesota

REFERENCES

Baron, R. A., & Gideon, D. M. (2000). Beyond social capital: How social skills can enhance entrepreneurs' success. *Academy of Management Executive (1993–2005), 14*(1), 106–116.

Côté, S., & Miners, C. T. H. (2006). Emotional intelligence, cognitive intelligence, and job performance. *Administrative Science Quarterly, 51*(1), 1–28.

Druskat, V., & Wolff, S. (2001). Building the emotional intelligence of groups. *Harvard Business Review,* 90.

Goleman, D. (1996). *Emotional intelligence: Why it can matter more than IQ.* New York: Bantam Books.

Hartley, D. (1999). Marketing and the 're-enchantment' of school management. *British Journal of Sociology of Education, 20*(3), 309–323.

Lippitt, R. (1939). Field theory and experiment in social psychology: Autocratic and democratic group atmospheres. *American Journal of Sociology, 45*(1), 26–49.

Maddock, M. (1990). *The heroine's journey: Women's quest for wholeness.* Boston: Shambala.

Osterman, K., & Kottkamp, R. (2004). *Reflective practice for educators.* Thousand Oaks, CA: Corwin.

Weick, K. E. (1993). The collapse of sensemaking in organizations: The Mann Gulch disaster. *Administrative Science Quarterly, 38*(4), 628–652.

NOTES

1. See also their book on reflective practice and educational leadership (Osterman & Kottkamp, 2004).

2. www.hartwickinstitute.org. I use their materials for students when I work with undergraduates, but not with doctoral students. Nevertheless, the teaching materials they provide are very helpful to the novice.

3. *Change: The Magazine of Higher Learning* is the functional equivalent of the *Phi Delta Kappan* periodical for higher education administrators.

4. Karen Seashore Louis served as director of the Center for Applied Research and Educational Improvement at the University of Minnesota, and department chair and associate dean of the College of Education and Human Development. Her research focuses on school improvement and reform, school effectiveness, leadership in school settings, and the politics of knowledge use in education.

Seashore Louis has been involved in applied policy and evaluation research for over thirty-five years. She is currently engaged in a collaborative evaluation of leadership and school-turnaround initiatives. Recent books include *Linking Leadership to Student Learning* (with Kenneth Leithwood, 2011), *Educational Policy: Political Culture and Its Effects* (2012), and *Cultivating Change in the Academy: Practicing the Art of Hosting Conversations That Matter within the University of Minnesota* (2013).

Seashore Louis is a fellow of the American Educational Research Association, where she also served as the president of Division A (Educational Administration). She is also an executive board member of the University Council for Educational Administration. Numerous awards received include the 2009 Campbell Lifetime Achievement Award from the University Council for Educational Administration.

Introduction

It is a rare occasion when in the process of conducting research it becomes a celebratory experience. This book is the result of that experience. It didn't start out that way. In the beginning we were simply curious. Inspired by Joseph Campbell, the guru of mythology, who revealed universal common threads in his groundbreaking classic *The Hero with a Thousand Faces* (1949), we felt compelled to discover if educational leaders were part of that mythology.

Let's be clear. Our research was not a plan to find educational heroes or heroines in our schools. We had little interest in the ideas of heroes or hero idolatry. The baggage of the "great leaders" in literature of the past is heavily masculine as some feminist critics have argued (e.g., Blackmore, 1999). Although we are often amused by the box-office success of blockbuster superhero films these days, we don't believe they have much to offer aspiring school leaders. We can't see Superman, Iron Man, or Cat Woman guiding colleagues in a sustained conversation to find an improved way to teach reading. And the notion of a superhero or heroine emancipating schools from oppressive forces would not even be the stuff of comic books.

But we, like Mohandas Gandhi, believe in courageous actions as the centerpiece of understanding effective leadership. Gandhi (as cited Iyer, 1973/2000) explicitly differentiated heroes from heroic action when he uttered, "We must worship heroism, not heroes. The hero may later on disgrace himself and in any case must cease to exist, but heroism is everlasting" (p. 138). Gandhi's own heroic actions, notably his leadership in propelling India toward independence, were arduous and dangerous, gritty and dispiriting. Much of his leadership journey was spent in jail. Many of his followers, unknown to us, also demonstrated heroic action.

What propelled our research was Campbell's (1949) leadership identity journey, something that struck us as applicable to educational leaders and their experiences of life and work. When Campbell described the characteristics of a "living mythology," he was referring to the stories that have sustained humans' trials and triumphs over many centuries. Evidenced by oral tradition, even pre-literate human societies told stories to explain, guide, and hearten them. At the heart of that struggle is the core of human identity.

The idea that identity is central to leadership has been well established by scholars (Bennis, 1989; Lumby & English, 2009; Mullen & Robertson, 2014; Papa, English, Davidson, Culver, & Brown, 2013). What we wanted to know was if educational leaders also saw themselves on such a journey and, if so, the meanings they attached to it. The call that awakens leaders might be to new tasks or dreams, such as to create their school as they would really want it to be, or to pursue forgotten dreams, such as to become an artist by learning to play a musical instrument.

Open-ended visual prompts with minimal structure served our study's purposes to explore mythic stories through graphic representation. In our interviews, we did not mention Campbell's work on mythology and the universal life journey but posed very general questions using five mythic life phases: the human condition, trials in life, human triumph, human transformation, and human crossing, with the addition of leadership as a dimension of the life-journey model.

The usual sort of paper-and-pencil survey was not going to work for our study. We did not want to place limits on the imagination, what Eisner (2002) identified as "complex and subtle forms of thinking" (pp. xi–xii). As Eisner, a leading scholar of arts-based educational research, described, new insight is gained when people create visual images or, in the case of our book, appreciatively scrutinize images, and in our approach specifically photographs.

One example of the creation of visual images is from Mullen's (1999) study of incarcerated females who produced drawings and narrative descriptions of universal symbols including the Hindu and Buddhist cultural image of the mandala. As explained by one participant, the mandala she drew was her personal vision of the human condition; this involved the struggle for wholeness depicted as the hands of her family members touching, but not her own. But hope, represented by a "spiritual sister," was available as one of the hands, albeit at a distance from her own. The artist "tattooed" powerful words, including "reaching out, help me" onto her drawing (Mullen, 1999, p. 157). In contrast, with surveys, respondents have been known to craft an unrealistically positive self-portrait. The same occurs with structured interviews.

What we learned from our study was simple yet profound. The educational leaders we brought into the open-ended interviews and our visual set-up knew that they would be reflecting on myth and experience in the life journey. While we thought that the journey motif was a powerful one in the human psyche, we were unprepared for the depth and emotionality of our respondents' stories. Even though in the past we have led numerous qualitative and quantitative studies, the use of photographic data as prompts for richness in storytelling was simply beyond what we could have imagined.

It strikes us that we have stumbled on a new fount in the way leadership studies can be pursued in the future. This finding is serendipitous. None of us had much inclination that would have prepared us for this realization at the time of the study. We think Einstein's reflection is apropos: "If we knew what it was we were doing, it would not be called research would it?" (Quote DB, 2009).

In the end, we found this study a celebration—of the human spirit, of a common humanity, and of a reaffirmation of educational leaders' commitment to helping children. We are all connected by our common ancestry and we were consistently reminded of that fact. The common humanity found in this research was unexpected.

As we contemplated the particular benefits of our study's content, scope, organization, and educational features, we discerned a practical curricular dimension. We hope educational leadership programs will benefit from the transdisciplinary and humanistic ideas portrayed in this work. We offer strategies for teaching, as well as experiencing, transdisciplinary and humanistic ideas about universal life journeys for educational leaders. We also critique the corporate-oriented leadership standards in our professional field that infuse curricula and courses. These standards have turned standardization, control, and—we contend—aesthetic deprivation into the "new normal."

This book can help with the search for wholeness in an education and policy context in which schools have been defined according to business efficacy values. As higher education faculty and mentors teach aspiring and practicing education leaders, alternatives to managerial values can be awakened. Efficiency day in and day out is the name of the game these days—managerial tasks have overtaken human and aesthetic values, reducing the ability of leaders to nurture the civic capacity of people in their milieu.

We are eager for leaders to stretch their imaginations and live more meaningfully beyond the daily grind. Actual practices of educational leadership involve artful performances—what Joseph Campbell might coin the creative imagination—with nuances and complexities derived from associative thinking, sensemaking, and human values and passions. We want to help illustrate the power of all of this.

With this work that is scholarly, not just practical, we present boundaries as porous and pursue possibilities beyond traditional scholarly communication in the educational leadership field. We see the work of mythologizing leadership, specifically at the intersection of universal narrative and educational leadership, as an attempt to break through disciplinary and ideological boundaries in the social sciences and educational leadership. Multidisciplinary work illustrates that leadership must become inclusive of many, even at times contradictory, perspectives.

The needs that we aim to satisfy are to empower leaders to operate in the light. To us, operating in the dark means denying one's potential to think artistically and in alternative ways that constrict vision and limit human potential.

Understanding the power of one's life in mythic terms can help leaders see more acutely, understand more deeply, and act more wisely. Campbell (2008) discussed the benefits of aliveness and exercising the creative imagination in doing this kind of work. Eisner (2002) encouraged the creation of aesthetic forms of experience in schools that "contribute to the growth of the person and mind" by animating "our imaginative capacities" and promoting "our ability to undergo emotionally pervaded experience" (p. xii).

This relatively short book endeavors to be provocative, expressive, informative, and scholarly, as well as boundary-spanning for the social sciences and humanities. We welcomed the academic freedom our publisher—Rowman & Littlefield Education—provided. We did not aspire to mold this particular work to the tight protocols of some book publishers. Educational leadership professors tend to prefer shorter works for students who work full time in school systems, so we kept this in mind as we crafted our book.

This is a contemporary take on Campbell's visionary work that is leadership oriented and multidisciplinary in a different way. *Myths to Live By* (1972/1993) and *The Hero with a Thousand Faces* (2008) were our touchstones. In these books, Campbell combined the insights of modern psychology with a revolutionary understanding of comparative mythology. His readers are from religion, anthropology, literature, and cinema.

Followers of Campbell who are intrigued by storytelling and the human condition may also find our work appealing or useful. Our unique contribution is to extend the life-journey motif into the educational leadership field from the perspectives of practicing school leaders and scholars. Campbell passed away a long time ago, but our work enlivens his in the context of leadership, which seems timely; also, our book is attuned to educational studies, matters of schooling, corporate influences in education, and the national policy landscape.

This is not a psychoanalytic text or a self-help guide, although readers might use it that way. Pearson's (1991, 1998) books are psychoanalytic self-help guides; these recognize the actions of preparing for a journey, taking the journey, and returning awakened. The fact that Pearson has been marketed to leadership groups only reinforces the need for a book that is written for educational leadership populations.

This book is organized to provide different entry points for the reader to make sense of our use of Campbell's model. The first part is essentially a sketch of the universal leadership journey that provides the big picture (chapter 1); then we move to seeing educational leaders on the journey, focusing on interpretation of the photographic data collected and analyzed (chapter 2). Following this, we present the unique nature of photographic data and show how the data connect to leadership storytelling; next we explore aspects of visual data, the culture of interpretation, and other issues based on the data from our study (chapter 3).

In chapter 4 we deal specifically with the data for leadership practice; here we describe the relevance for such practice by examining what we have learned about how leaders actually practice in schools today. Finally, in chapter 5 we reveal relevance for research and preparation by identifying the relevance of our study. We call for spending more time in these areas on the identity construction of leaders around core values. (The key terms in each chapter are identified and defined at the end of each chapter.)

It is our hope that this initial study will be a stimulus for more to follow in which the human side of leadership is more fully explored and deeply appreciated. We see creative connections with the arts and humanities as that unfolds, and we see educational leaders in the forefront of that movement. It's time for their real artistry and power to be revealed.

Chapter One

Sketching the Universal Leadership Journey

Educational leadership is a specific role within an institutional setting, but also a supreme moral duty within the confines of American jurisprudence, history, and idealism. While schools are mired in the bells and whistles of daily schedules and curricular and extracurricular activities, on a deeper level they represent a moral compass that transmits values, beliefs, and ethics. There is nothing scientific or neutral about this cultural process of schooling. Schools sit at the apex of the most dearly held values and beliefs of American life. Within a democracy these values and beliefs are constantly being tested.

The discourse about educational leadership has been dominated by concerns about management from the organizational level to the classroom level. Managerial thinking has a long history within the profession, beginning with the doctrines of "scientific management" advanced by Frederick Taylor, a mechanical engineer focused on industrial efficiency in the early 1900s (Lumby & English, 2010).

Over the past century, Taylor's influence has slowly morphed into today's preoccupation with high-stakes testing, the rating of schools by test scores, and pay for the performance of teachers and administrators. You can see this managerial mantra in school reform policies and the U.S. legislative mandates No Child Left Behind and Race to the Top, as well as countless other state initiatives (Lumby & English, 2010; Tienken & Orlich, 2013).

National and state standards for educational leadership also reflect this preoccupation with management tasks. These form the "how-to" dimensions of skills required to implement what is believed to be the route to success for all children, though the evidence that they will accomplish that goal does not mean it will happen anytime soon if at all. Clearly something critical is missing.

In this book, *The Leadership Identity Journey: An Artful Reflection*, we posit that the bedrock of educational leadership is the identity of the leader him- or herself. Who *is* this person called leader? The leadership journey occurs within the day-to-day terrain of leading schools, and it encompasses complex challenges that are psycho-emotional as well as personal, cultural, and historical.

Indeed, leadership *is* a journey, and it is this compelling metaphor that informed this work. Before leaders can attract and educate potential followers, they must engage in the ongoing, challenging construction of themselves; for, as American scholar and pioneer of the educational leadership field Warren Bennis (1989) poignantly observed over ten years ago, "Leaders have nothing but themselves to work with" (p. 47).

We have employed one of the most compelling leadership-journey models from the pioneering work of American mythologist Joseph Campbell (1972/1993) who first described it in *The Hero with a Thousand Faces*. Campbell's desire was to identify universal themes within the panoply of mythological narratives that span Western and Eastern cultures.

Within these narratives Campbell found patterns or archetypes, as Swiss psychiatrist Carl Jung (1967) called them. These archetypes are the resilient, deep roots of the human psyche that percolate within every human being's unique and personal life journey. They comprise the "basic images of ritual, mythology, and vision" and "are directly valid for all mankind" (Campbell, 2008, p. 19). The journey leaders take or accept is qualitatively unique, say, in contrast with those of teachers, because the outcomes enable them to inspire and move others toward common goals at a larger scale.

Campbell's *leadership journey* is shown in figure 1.1.

The leadership journey involves various parts. We next describe these in broad terms to lay the groundwork for discussing the dimensions in greater detail.

THE CALL

The call represents an event, an initial awareness of something or someone. It could be an unsuspecting turn, as in a strange occurrence, a door opened that was unplanned, a puzzlement of some kind. In some narratives, the call comes as a blunder of some kind, a wrong road taken or an accidental happening. It evokes images of dark forests, fog-enclosed harbors, overgrown gardens, unfinished bridges, and other mysterious scenes.

According to Campbell (1973) the call is "the awakening of the self" (p. 51), a kind of wake-up call. To that effect, American writer John Gardner (1963) remarked, "More often than not we don't want to know ourselves, don't want to depend on ourselves, don't want to live with ourselves. By

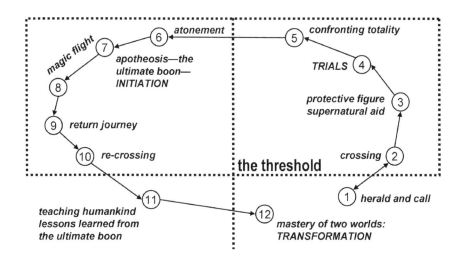

Figure 1.1. **Critical Demarcations in *Campbell's* Universal Leadership Journey**

middle life most of us are accomplished fugitives from ourselves" (p. 13). It takes courage to come to grips with the question of identity and who we are becoming in the face of struggle and adversity, and not everyone heeds the call.

Campbell was highly influenced by C. G. Jung (1958), who also observed that "man is an enigma to himself" and "knows how to distinguish himself from the other animals in point of anatomy and physiology, but as a conscious, reflecting being, gifted with speech, he lacks all criteria for self-judgment" (pp. 55–56). At the bottom, accepting the leadership journey is a quest for self-understanding and identity, and identity is the beginning of the construction of the concept of self (Lumby & English, 2009). However, identity shifting often occurs in response to political pressures or as an enactment of profound personal change (Mullen & Robertson, 2014).

THE HERALD AND THE CROSSING

After the call there is the appearance of a herald, a protective figure of some sort, often weird and supernatural. Many tales sport a fairy godmother or guardian angel to accompany one on a journey that involves the crossing into unfamiliar territory. In Jungian terms, this is equated with the unconscious, which is very threatening because it, too, is deep and unknown.

Campbell (1973) indicated in many myths that the submersion of the traveler into the belly of the whale is the symbolic crossing into the unknown. Another way of thinking about the presence of a herald is the great teachers of the world's religions. Examples include Buddha, Jesus, Mohammed, and the ancient Chinese sages.

Albert Schweitzer (1965), theologian/humanitarian, also pondered crossing: "As soon as man does not take his existence for granted, but beholds it as something unfathomably mysterious thought begins" (p. 33). Existence has a mystery all its own. He also observed that "thought has a dual task to accomplish: to lead us out of a naive and into a profounder affirmation of life and the universe" (p. 33). To behold mystery take one step, and to affirm it take another.

TRIALS

In universal narrative, trials are often physical tasks, sometimes mental mazes and riddles that must be solved. In this phase of the leadership journey the leader is aided by a protective figure who bestows secret keys and esoteric knowledge to mount and defeat obstacles that stand in the way. What stands in the way might be or include the attitudes or ideologies of the traveler. While trials along the leadership journey are often expressed as external challenges, most are actually internal. For example, a profound fear of bullies might actually manifest as bullying behavior in others—the lines blur between internal and external trials.

CONFRONTING REALITY

In this phase of the journey, the leader comes to see contradictions in him- or herself and the world. The traveler confronts reality, or is confronted by reality, and wrestles with what is unresolved. To perceive clearly the nature of things is often painful, and many people decide they do not want to see things as they are, or they refuse. French writer/philosopher Albert Camus (as cited in Zaretsky, 2010) observed, "I have no wish to lie or to be lied to. I want to keep my lucidity to the last, and gaze upon my death with all the fullness of my jealousy and horror" (p. 159). This is admirable—to want to be fully conscious and exposed so as to feel the truth and fullness of human emotions.

The reality of the world and what comprises it must be thoroughly comprehended. We must feel compelled to look more deeply and thereby extend our perceptual reach. Gardner (1969) spoke of this challenge when he candidly observed that

> moral seriousness does not resolve complex problems; it only impels us to face
> the problems rather than run away. Clearheadedness does not slay dragons; it

only spares us the indignity of fighting paper dragons while the real ones are breathing down our necks. But those are not trivial advantages. (p. 167)

One person's paper dragon might be another person's real one. If your colleague's paper dragon is the unfairness of his or her salary as compared with others, your real dragon might be the neglect or abuse of children within your school community. A dragon does not need to be breathing down our neck to be simmering within us or to be summoned up from the past—and with a vengeance and a fury.

ATONEMENT

This phase of the journey is a reconciliation, the triumph of love over hate, and the erasure of prejudice and other traditions to find ultimate meaning. The traveler will feel a deep sense of satisfaction by, for example, making amends or reparation for an inquiry or a wrong with another human being. (In Christianity, this process extends to humans and God.)

But to participate in this triumph, the leader must confront personal flaws, superstitions, and vanities. For example, Mother Teresa (as cited in Benenate, 1997) viewed service above self and said this of herself: "I must be willing to give whatever it takes to do good to others. This requires that I be willing to give until it hurts. Otherwise, there is no true love in me and I bring injustice, not peace, to those around me" (p. 49).

Robert Greenleaf (as cited in Frick, 2004), originator of the concept of servant leadership, spoke of *entheos*, a sixteenth-century word with *en* meaning "possessed of" and *theos* meaning "spirit." He described his insight, or atonement using the word *entheos* and its association with "being inspired" as by spirit. His explanation was that to be strong we must choose "the right aim" and pursue it over time and, for this journey, "one must have inspiration backed by power" (p. 233).

APOTHEOSIS AND THE ULTIMATE BOON

Apotheosis for leaders means being exalted to a special rank or stature or to experience being elevated to a transcendent position. Not about promotion on the career ladder, this stage represents a new state of awareness, an understanding and a profound transformation, and a final evolution. It signifies a person's erasure of ego.

Without ego, new insights arrive. These bring happiness, peace, and an appreciation of the rhythms and meanings of life. Many kinds of apotheosis are possible on the leadership journey. Bringing out the best in others is at the core of personal transformation, which is quintessentially spiritual. Vaill

(1989) said that "all true leadership is indeed spiritual leadership": "The reason is that beyond everything else that can be said about it, leadership is concerned with bringing out the best in people," and "one's best is tied intimately to one's deepest sense of oneself, to one's spirit" (p. 224). The leader who is the apotheosis of compassion will have this deep connection to others and the self, as will the leader who is the apotheosis of integrity and certainly of wisdom.

In *Extraordinary Minds* American psychologist Howard Gardner (1997) summarized lessons learned from examining Mozart, Freud, Virginia Woolf, and Mahatma Gandhi's lives. While these great minds suffered losses and defeats on their personal journeys, they all were able to overcome "asynchronies" and, moreover, "reframe frustrations as opportunities, and above all, persevere" (p. 135). The ultimate boon (or benefit bestowed on leaders) is a coagulum of spirit, challenge, and persistence. Spirit itself functions as a kind of binding agent for leaders who operate from the core belief that service to humankind is above self.

MAGIC FLIGHT AND THE RETURN

Once insights of the most penetrating manner are attained, the leader must return to the world, to her community and society. The leader must now bring this new awareness to others. In short, the leader must teach from the lessons learned during personal transformation.

Leadership is ultimately about teaching. A cogent example can be found in Greenleaf's life. He initiated the servant leadership movement and founded the Greenleaf Center for Servant Leadership. His key message was that authentic listening takes time and effort and that *leadership can be taught.*

Greenleaf's servant-oriented perspective arose out of his journey as a Quaker, which nurtured his acceptance of persons with unlimited liability, openness to novelty, and development of strength based on *entheos* (spirit). Leading as a servant, Greenleaf also learned how to listen. Listening, while a crucial skill for a business executive, had to be active and engaged, which is different from passive receptivity to a message.

RECROSSING

This stage marks the leader's return to the squabble and cacophony, pain and predicaments of the society left behind. Any temptation to withdraw from this return must be resisted and the new responsibilities accepted. A good example of a recrossing is Gandhi's march to the sea to make salt. Gandhi had spent years in jail, writing and reflecting and later working in villages in

India. At last he believed India was ready to challenge British rule militantly but nonviolently.

The march was two hundred miles long, and Gandhi's fellow walkers were well prepared. Gandhi, over sixty years of age, walked twelve miles a day for twenty-four days. At the end of the march, the travelers all took salt from the Indian Ocean in defiance of the British-imposed salt tax and the subsequent monopoly on salt itself. The British responded violently, jailing over fifty thousand Indians for their defiance.

When at last the British reviewed their own actions, Gandhi was invited to talk with the viceroy. Handed a cup of tea, "he poured a bit of salt (tax-free) into it out of a small paper bag hidden in his shawl and remarked smilingly, 'to remind us of the famous Boston Tea Party'" (as cited in Erikson, 1969, p. 448). With wit and wisdom, Gandhi had indeed engaged in recrossing.

TEACHING AND MASTERY OF THE WORLD

A major problem facing the returning leader involves translating what has been learned into language and understandable examples that are communicative. Metaphorically, it may well have signified what Jesus said when he told his followers, "So I tell you, ask—it'll be given to you; seek—you'll find; knock—it'll be opened for you. Rest assured: everyone who asks receives; everyone who seeks finds; and for the one who knocks it is opened" (Funk, Hoover, & the Jesus Seminar, 1993, p. 328).

This is sound advice for someone who has undergone the leadership journey: Self-development is a path open to all seekers. We must be constantly growing ourselves if we are to teach and lead effectively and especially inspire others. As Greenleaf said, "The leader must be a growing person. Non-growth people are finding it more and more difficult to lead, especially to lead young people" (cited in Frick, 2004, p. 271).

TRANSFORMATION

This stage is where the leader negotiates the external and internal world and where tension arises. The external world is a place of confusion, conflict, pain, death, and life. The internal world, which intersects with the external world, occupies a life of its own. The leader understands earthly issues and their importance but does not accept injustices and social inequities. If anything, there is a deepened sense of resolve to address them.

This is neither a laid-back type of acceptance nor simply a more caring stance toward others, including oppressed citizens. Rather, this is an attitude that rejects injustices and social inequities, and the postponement to strive to resolve them. Egoless and transformed, the leader exhibits the agency s/he wants to see in others and in situations. Greenleaf aptly remarked: "Everything begins with the individual as 'in here, not out there'" (cited in Frick, 2004, p. 348).

We pause to think of Lutheran pastor Tom Preston (2011), who described a ten-day walking trip through Italy where he took the time to learn to see and listen again. At the end of his journey by the sea and through small towns he wrote,

> It had taken me a long time to see how much I tend to control situations or people, although I think I am trying to better the situation. Letting people be as they are, instead of wanting to change and judge them, stems from my journey, of learning to remain in my own skin—to remain on my side of the fence as it were. It starts with me. (p. 123)

Preston's internal world shifted—maybe tilted!—upon realizing that he needed to let go of the need to control external forces, specifically by judging people instead of allowing them to be. His personal change deepened as he gained awareness of how he had been doing this and of the kind of person he wanted to become. Writing about this process presented an opportunity for teaching others about what he had learned and how he had changed as a result.

IT'S NOT ABOUT HERO WORSHIP

All human beings undergo a journey—it is inevitable in the act of living, but experiencing it mindfully is another matter. The language of Campbell's (2008) *The Hero with a Thousand Faces* affords a key for unlocking the languages used to symbolize and discuss it.

Leaders, like us, are human beings. They travel the same roads, suffer defeats, and confront problems inherent in the human situation. They experience disappointment—lose their way, and are hurt by what happens to them or others. Ackerman and Maslin-Ostrowski (2002) described "wounded leaders": "Wounding is an inevitable part of leadership; it might have to be considered part of the job. It seems virtually impossible to avoid wounding, if one chooses such an approach, then that too is a wound" (p. 10).

Out of the hurt and pain, educational leaders grow, but they must take risks. Risk-averse leaders and those who are conflict avoidant are not likely to grow. Insulating themselves and withdrawing from the world, they cannot effectively lead people who want to grow. Conflict is built into relationships and leadership, and it exists within the fiber of our being. Leaders are human, and there will be times when they fail or feel that they have.

It's not *if* leaders will fail—it's *when* they fail. And it's more than just learning how to survive the failures that may be individual, cultural, or organizational. It's about finding growth in failure to reassess, to become better and stronger, and, we contend, that much more compassionate as someone who leads with integrity and who seeks wisdom.

Popular books about failure not being an option for leaders and anyone else are bunk, we think. If Edison had to be right the first time with the light bulb we'd still be using candles. Failure is part of living, part of learning. And it's part of getting up, stretching beyond our comfort zone, and moving on. Just as failure can be attached to an individual, it can be attached to an organization, system, or culture. Regardless, it feels personal and involves humans taking action or inaction—striving or closing down.

Our use of Campbell's universal leadership journey was neither to find heroes nor to create them. Instead, we aspired to understand how leaders experienced the journeys that have shaped them, molded their identities, and helped them succeed. *Heroic action* is possible along the journey and in retrospect through teaching.

And we were not about hero worship either and we agree with Clarence Lusane (as cited in Nguyen, 2010), a scholar who observed, "What is needed is not so much charismatic leaders as ordinary people rising to meet the extraordinary challenges of their time" (p. 197). Ordinary people can become extraordinary leaders. And that's the importance of the leadership journey. It is the journey's transformative power we wanted to tap into when we began this research.

FROM THE MEEK TO THE MIGHTY

Placing the Campbell leadership journey in modern times (leaving the realm of myth for the moment), we offer a real-life example: Mohandas Gandhi (1869–1948). His early life was undistinguished and by some standards almost pathetic. It would have been difficult to discern any extraordinary powers. He was far from the "Great Soul" of India.

As Fisher (1950) tells the story, Gandhi was the fourth child of his father's fourth and last marriage. By his own account, Gandhi was a mediocre student. He was so shy he would run home after school for fear of having to talk to anyone or meet other males who might mock him. At school, he once was beaten by the teacher and "wept piteously" (as cited in Fisher, p. 19). At twelve, he stole cigarettes from his parents, and a year later he was married by compact with another family to Kasturbai, who was the same age.

Gandhi considered himself a coward. He even kept his light on at night for fear of ghosts and serpents. Since his family members were strictly vegetarian, Gandhi secretly ate meat. He tried for a year to restrain himself and reproached himself for it later, as well as for lying about it.

After Gandhi stole jewelry from his older brother, he encountered a profound moral dilemma. To deal with it he wrote an exhaustive confession and presented it to his father. He asked to be punished, promised to never steal again, and pleaded with his father that he not blame himself for his son's wrongful actions. Surprisingly, his father cried after reading the letter; he tore it up and lay down on the bed. Gandhi wept too.

Gandhi left India for England to study law. Because of a vow he had made to his mother at nineteen years of age, he refused to eat meat. Consequently, he went hungry much of the time. Withdrawn, he was too shy to ask for more bread when served at the table (Gandhi, 2008). A new persona emerged when, in London, Gandhi tried to become a perfect "English gentleman." He bought new clothes, wore a gold watch chain, learned to tie a tie, donned a stove pipe hat, took dancing lessons, tried to play the violin, and learned some French. But three months later he gave all of this up.

In the words of biographer and grandson Rajmohan Gandhi (2008), "Mahatmas was sensing that not a personality but an inner firmness was what he needed to develop; not a power to charm or impress with figure or voice, but an internal spirit that holds on to a goal" (p. 31). As Campbell (2008) described with the universal journey metaphor, the journey always involves an internal battle. Gandhi experienced a profound struggle in his spiritual development.

Gandhi's inability to stray from the truth was revealed while he was in London and had occasion to meet English girls, including a much younger girl. He did not tell her he was married, but later confessed, "I did not hesitate to pass myself off as a bachelor" (Gandhi, 2008, p. 34). However, when he sensed things were getting more serious, he wrote her, explaining that not only was he married but he also had a son. The young girl responded almost immediately to his "frank" letter and forgave him. They became friends.

The time in England was formative for the young Gandhi. He had concluded that God really did exist. He became active in the English vegetarian movement, where he was exposed to politics, writing nine articles for a newsletter. He learned how to organize meetings, mobilize people, and develop a political agenda, all skills that would amplify in his days in India and South Africa. But he had a persistent problem with public speaking, which felt painfully awkward.

After returning to India, Gandhi had trouble attracting clients to his law practice. And in his first case, he became so frightened of speaking that he could not cross-examine some witnesses. He would sit in silence, return the fee to the client, and leave the courtroom. Not an auspicious beginning for an up-and-coming barrister, wouldn't you say? Bored with his life in India,

Gandhi accepted an offer to go to South Africa. He served as a go-between for a large firm that spanned Indian and European branches on an important case.

Gandhi's Threshold and Crossing

Gandhi's crossing (on the way to South Africa) involved a humiliating experience: After he purchased a first-class ticket, he was thrown off the train. The reason? "Colored passengers" could not occupy the elite cabins. If he had accepted being reassigned to a third-class compartment he would have remained on the train, but he refused; the police were called, and he was rudely deposited in the cold of the night.

This episode marked Gandhi's crossing. Gandhi (1948), shivering through the night, was shocked at the treatment he received, later writing in his autobiography:

> I began to think of my duty. Should I fight for my rights or go back to India, or should I go on to Pretoria without minding the insults, and return to India after finishing the case? It would be cowardice to run back to India without fulfilling my obligation. The hardship to which I was subjected was superficial— only a symptom of the deep disease of colour prejudice. I should try if possible to root out the disease and suffer hardships in the process. Redress for wrongs I should seek only to the extent that would be necessary for the removal of the colour prejudice. (p. 141)

Enraged, Gandhi determined to answer the call of racial prejudice against Indians in South Africa. He did not want to be a coward any longer. He felt strongly pulled at, through a rude awakening that he personally endured, to make a difference for people of color who were suffering hardships. In this goal he was aided by more than one protective figure on his leadership journey.

Gandhi's Protective Figures

First, there was Baker, who found him a place to stay since lodging was very poor and limited for a colored person. Then there was Sheth Tyeb Haji Khan Muhammad, a wealthy Muslim businessperson, and other contacts who formed a protective shield around Gandhi. Gandhi made many friends and created groups that befriended financial backers. In India his friendship with one protective figure was instrumental.

Trials

Gandhi discovered that Indians in South Africa were stigmatized "coolies" and that they were often confined to "coolie locations," basically ghettoes.

Wherever he went and whatever he did he was constantly reminded of the prevalent racism against Indians in South Africa. Indians had to pay a special poll tax. Indians could not vote. And Indians were prohibited from being on public walkways after 9:00 p.m. without a permit. Motivated to work as a lawyer on their behalf, Gandhi made himself into a competent attorney who stood up for social justice causes.

Confronting Reality

Within a social system built on racial and class divisions, Gandhi carefully picked his fights. His strategy was not to directly attack racial prejudice, believing that the desired change in laws would "yield only to patient toil and education" (as cited in Fischer, 1950, p. 48).

Gandhi's attention was focused on the laws and making these just. He understood that White people would also have the upper hand in the larger community because of the superior social position they held. Making legal fairness his conduit for change, he argued that all people within the British empire were bound by the same laws. He reasoned that if all stood equal before the law, human concern would be resolved over time.

Atonement

The unification of the leader and a higher calling in Gandhi's case was his creation of a new way of grasping equality and fairness. The development of satyagraha, a catalytic idea binding justice and love, was slow in coming; it arose out of the Hindu idea of self-purification. After running an ad in his newspaper requesting help in naming his concept, Gandhi settled on the term *satyagraha*, *sat* meaning "truth" and *agraha* meaning "firmness."

Satyagraha became the symbol of the struggle for equality and fairness. Biographer Louis Fischer (1950) commented on satyagraha as a counterforce in the struggle against systemic racism. Quoting Gandhi, Fischer wrote, "If words fail to convince the adversary perhaps purity, humility, and honesty will. The opponent must be 'weaned from error by patience and sympathy,' weaned, not crushed; converted, not annihilated" (p. 77).

Satyagraha also stood for peacefulness, truth, and love and for a common humanity achieved through deliberate struggle and education, not war. Education is the teacher. Gandhi (as cited in Iyer, 1993) identified satyagraha as spirituality or "soul-force" and truth as "the very substance of the soul," explaining, "That is why this force is called *satyagraha*. The soul is informed with knowledge. In it burns the flame of love. If someone gives us pain through ignorance, we shall win him through love" (p. 309).

From this perspective, atonement is the unification of action and love, and force is a necessary action and love, a desirable bond.

Apotheosis

As a nation-building leader, Gandhi eventually came to understand that racial prejudice involved conflict on multiple fronts, not just the legal front. One of his biographers, Lelyveld (2011), remarked, "To say that Gandhi wasn't absolutely consistent isn't to convict him of hypocrisy; it's to acknowledge that he was a political leader preoccupied with the task of building a nation, or sometimes just holding it together" (p. 225).

Gandhi's campaign of satyagraha involved civil disobedience, untouchability, hygiene, sanitation, education, and women's rights, including "the right of widows to remarry and the abolition of child marriage" (Lelyveld, 2011, p. 226). Again, it took force to generate praxis and a new vision.

The Return Journey

Gandhi (as cited in Lelyveld, 2011) took a skeptical view of his life's work, remarking that for men like himself, "you have to measure them not by the rare moments of greatness in their lives, but by the amount of dust they collect on their feet in the course of life's journey" (p. 226). Leaders collect dust on their feet and for them personal greatness is not the goal.

Gandhi (as cited in Attenborough, 1982) also demurred that he had "nothing new to teach the world," reasoning that "truth and nonviolence are as old as the hills. All I have done is to try experiments in both on as vast as scale as I could" (p. 10). Gandhi was humble about what he had to teach but believed it was the highest form of truth. Going on campaigns to spread truth and nonviolence for the betterment of humanity means having a deep belief in your message and dusty feet from well-worked trails.

Transformation

Completely reconstructing himself in his struggles in South Africa and India, Gandhi thought of himself as a realist. Yet he imagined the world a better place and worked tirelessly to remake it into something better. Consider the scale of his work—above self-interest and far beyond only a few beneficiaries. Ponder the level of risk involved—very high possibility for failure, with many "opportunities" to fail along the way. Social transformation arose out of his long-time suffering at the heels of his own misfortune and vision to make a cruel world humane.

Reflecting on his triumphs, Gandhi (as cited in Attenborough, 1982) wrote, "I have not the shadow of a doubt that any man or woman can achieve what I have, if he or she would make the same effort and cultivate the same hope and faith" (p. 10). Certainly Gandhi's journey demonstrates that not all leaders are exceptional at the outset of their journey, but they may become extraordinary—their feet walk in the same dust as everyone else's.

SO WHAT *IS* LEADERSHIP?

As many readers are aware, the leadership literature has a huge reservoir of definitions of leadership (see Rost, 1991). In some ways it's akin to the common cold: Everyone has had one, but the medical profession seems baffled on how to deal with them, so if you have one you end up buying over-the-counter remedies that only treat symptoms.

Our definition of leadership lies within the scope of Campbell's universal journey. This is consistent with the notion that all people are on a journey in the process of living their lives. It seems like some people never receive a "call" and if they did they might not recognize it or respond to it. There might not be a protective figure in their lives and, in other cases, the trials may overwhelm the traveler instead of helping shape the individual. They might break down or burn out or their system might. Within the journey experience there can be difficult decisions (e.g., involving moral conflict and power) to be made that do not always lead to an apotheosis.

So nothing is assured in the journey, just as nothing is assured in life itself. French philosopher Albert Camus understood this so very well, as noted by biographer Robert Zaretsky (2010): "We are overmatched and inevitably overwhelmed in this struggle, but this is not cause for despair. . . . True despair occurs only when 'we no longer know the reasons for struggling, or if it is even necessary to struggle'" (pp. 159–160). As leaders we very well can feel overmatched and overwhelmed. Despair and struggle go hand-in-hand in many cases along the way. Avoid giving up. True despair means abandonment of the experience of the struggle that in itself is a lubricant for taking the journey.

Leadership is a journey, first about self and self-knowledge, then the struggle to deal with the obstacles in our lives. In schools, the paramount conflicts are moral in nature, even if it is under the surface. School leaders stand at the apex of those conflicts where their values and beliefs are constantly being tested, and possibly formed or reformed.

Leadership, then, is about seeking resolution, finding commonalities, working for consensus, constructing coalitions, teaching, and educating deeply and broadly. And teaching isn't hectoring, preaching, and just talking—it's about listening respectfully and with an open mind to all parties involved. It's also about creating an atmosphere in which trust takes root and flourishes so that humanity can be united through compassion, integrity, and wisdom.

In short, leadership is about *becoming*. It's not the arrival that matters so much—it's the journey itself. Gandhi (as cited in Attenborough, 1982) said it best: "Joy lies in the fight, in the attempt, in the suffering involved, not in the victory itself" (p. 13). Accepting the call to carry out a mission of goodwill is celebratory in and of itself, as is moving through all the journey's phases.

THE PROJECT OF THIS BOOK

Using Campbell's vision of the universal leadership journey, we set forth to explore if educational leaders follow such a journey and are aware of its importance and ripple effects; and if they are, what that might tell us about leaders and leadership, and the dynamics of experiencing and developing, understanding and transforming in their lives.

Our study of educational leaders revolved around these questions:

1. Do leaders follow something akin to a leadership journey as described by Campbell (2008) in *The Hero with a Thousand Faces?* Do they see themselves on a journey of growth and development, as human beings and as leaders?
2. If leaders intuit that their life and work are on a path, does it connect to Campbell's description of the universal mythic pattern? If so, what are some possibilities for reimagining leadership, conducting research, and preparing future educational leaders?

We started with the key assumptions that follow about leadership—that it is a social construct, is situated culturally, and often invokes heroic action.

Leadership Is a Social Construct

We rejected the long-held bias that leaders are born rather than made. We eschewed genetic- or trait-based approaches to defining and pigeon-holing leadership. In the case of Gandhi and most other leaders, leadership emerges from a process of creating one's identity and constructing the self.

Leadership Is Situated Culturally

While there may be certain universal themes in the development of leaders, as Campbell (2008) has described, leadership as a transformational process occurs within cultural traditions. These include specific symbols, particular modes of communication, and shared stories that bind leaders and followers.

Leadership Invokes Heroic Action

Gandhi emphatically denied that he was a hero of any kind. He eschewed the idea that leaders must be or ought to be considered heroes. Rather, he affirmed heroic action. Courageous action for the right moral cause moved Gandhi.

Similarly, we posit that educational leaders toiling in school communities day in and day out must also exhibit heroic action. As Gandhi (as cited in Iyer, 1973/2000) observed, "A leader is only first among equals. Someone may be put first, but he is no stronger than the weakest link in the chain" (p. 139). The proverbial expression "a chain is no stronger than its weakest link" means that leaders are not superior but are part of a group, and collectively the strength of leadership is tested by the weakest person who can damage a culture or negatively affect desired outcomes.

Wisdom in leadership means exhibiting the attributes of a chain—strength, integrity, and dependability—and encouraging one's followers to be strong links that hoist up the tasks that need to be done. The power of the leader is not absolute. The effectiveness of the leader emanates from the strength of the people s/he is leading. If the people have self-doubt, or are fearful and insecure, the leader can be that much more effective by leading alongside and by following. Sending powerful messages of unity can create cohesion and purpose.

HOW WE DID THIS STUDY

For this book we tested Campbell's concept of the leadership journey. We sought to understand possibilities for its representation in the quest for identity and competence in the process of becoming an educational leader. Accordingly, we determined not to just directly ask potential respondents about such a journey. We did not want to assess the journey by "leading the witness," that is, by giving away the expected answer. We had a strong desire to use visual data of a more interpretative type that could evoke meaning-making.

Deciding to use distinctive photographs, we grouped the images into the phases of Campbell's leadership journey (see figure 1.1). The photographs were evocative and visually striking, as well as open-ended.

The Sample

We conducted one-on-one interviews with eleven males and females, White and African American. They were assistant principals, principals, and district leaders in K–12 public school districts across grade levels. Three of the school principals were at the elementary level, one was at the secondary level, and another worked with grades 3–12. Three high school assistant principals also participated, as did two district leaders and a project coordinator. Participants held a master's degree in educational leadership, and some were working on the doctorate. This sample was balanced in gender but not ethnicity.

Because our target was practicing leaders, and because a snowball strategy was used to identify a purposeful sample, a White male majority surfaced, with two professionals of color included. Our take on the commonly used snowball strategy in qualitative research, as described by Miles and Huberman (1994), was to access our hard-to-find population by inviting initial leaders who agreed to take part in the research to help identify others who may have been willing to take part.

While we strove for variability in gender and race, eligibility for participation was simply current leadership at the school or district level. The sample we selected allowed for physical access to practicing school leaders, even though it involved long car rides. We scheduled after-school times for our participants and met them in a convenient location.

For this study we avoided turning to our own students and employees, and anyone with whom we had an association of any kind. Thus, we monitored power dynamics in our roles as professors while attempting to establish a feeling of safety for the participants.

Potential respondents received an e-vite and information about the study in general terms but not the interview protocol itself. This strategy was used to help practitioners decide whether to share their thoughts in an interview without disclosing the questions that would be asked or identifying the photographs that would be used.

We were determined to steer clear of prepackaged responses in the interview sessions. Instead, we set our bar at eliciting spontaneous, creative reactions to the question prompts and photos. No incentives (e.g., monetary compensation) were offered. Participants were informed that if they experienced discomfort at any point during the study or interview, they were free to exit. All were assured anonymity. On several grounds, the spirit of volunteerism was intact.

Interview Procedures

Each digitally taped interview lasted around 60 minutes, totaling 660 minutes. One of us would take extensive notes on a laptop while another researcher would verbally provide the prompts and clarifications and handle the stacks of photographs. Participants were interviewed in person by Carol Mullen and Fenwick English before or after their work day. They were not given a copy of the interview prompts or photos. Instead, they were challenged to be creative in the moment in their ability to explore evocative visuals, universal themes, and lived experience and to possibly make organic connections based on the photographs.

In this private space, participants encountered three stacks of photographs from which they were prompted to make a selection *and* verbally give a rationale for the choice. Next, they were asked to identify the photos that best represent the human condition. After that we asked the same about human triumph over life's obstacles, followed by human transformation, the human crossing, and leadership.

The interview protocol listed question prompts we had developed based on our understanding of Campbell's journey stages (see the section in chapter 2 titled "Probing the Inner World of Educational Leaders," for the verbatim protocol). The majority of the talking in every interview was done by the participants. This was important to us—we wanted to be listening and learning.

Artistic Treatment

The photos we decided on depict a range of events and periods in American and world history, and emotive pictures around life's important events (loss, death, struggle, etc.). We made selections that suggestively reflected or even matched Campbell's life journey stages.

We were "testing" Campbell's vision, so we needed visual images that came across as emotional and powerful. Because people's cultural conditioning says a lot about what they see in photos, or art for that matter (see, e.g., Sontag, 1977), we wanted strong cues, not right answers. And the photos did just that.

The journey life-phases and representative photos (i.e., the most popular ones selected based on our data interpretation) appear in table 1.1.

The photographs were arranged in three stacks of eleven. Table 1.1 shows the first, second, and third choices the respondents made across all five of Campbell's stages, as well as the general leadership category. It is from these data that our interpretations were constructed.

Data Interpretation

Data were sorted according to these nonidentifiers: participant demographics, state, current professional role, professional background and goals, academic degrees, and, importantly, types of statements made relative to the journey motif. Carol and Fenwick independently coded the data. Major themes corresponding with Campbell's mythic phases—human condition, trials in life, human triumph, human transformation, and human crossing— were identified.

The sixth phase was the general concept of "leadership" across all the categories but still within Campbell's framework. We used a combinational distributive and numerical analysis for each of the six variables. After computing numerical outcomes for the demographic and photographic information, we analyzed the recorded responses by identifying key words and phrases (Miles & Huberman, 1994), accomplishing interpretive coherence (Smith, Miller-Kahn, Heinecke, & Jarvis, 2004).

This approach involved a deliberate choice not to go down well-worn, checklist-driven paths in leadership research. We did not endeavor to devel-

Table 1.1.   Phases of the Universal Life Journey and Representative Photos

Phase 1: Human Condition	African Americans walking along riverside
Phase 2: Trials in Life	Coffin in the Andes Worried woman in the Depression
Phase 3: Human Triumph	Coffin in the Andes Worried woman in the Depression
Phase 4: Human Transformation	Nazi soldiers marching African American politician Woman's faces Woman pointing to her eye
Phase 5: Human Crossing	Comedian-satirist giving the finger Worried woman in the Depression Pensive woman
Phase 6 (added): Leadership	Man framing something in making a film

op or use the usual checklists based on behavioral assumptions that frequently appear in existing literature (e.g., Kouzes & Posner, 2002; Shipman, Queen, & Peel, 2007).

We chose an approach that reconnects the arts and humanities with the sciences, heeding the advice of scholar Heilbrunn (1996) to explore issues of mystery in leadership and philosophical thinking about existence. To grow the study of leadership as a discipline, we "will have to cast a wider net"; when you really think about it, Heilbrunn must have been onto something when she wrote that "the most important things about leadership lie far beyond the capabilities of science to analyze" (p. 11).

Assumptions about what constitutes a "scientific study" of leaders limit what can be discovered about leadership because much of what makes a leader successful is eliminated at the outset by the theoretical lens selected to study it (see English, 2007). The approach we selected for this study reflects our attempt to expand the lens to include more of what comprises leadership, such as mystery, philosophy, and spirituality.

Campbell (1990) said it cogently when he remarked,

> We now come to the business of finding the fire in yourself. It's a psychological act of discriminating between the physical transforming aspect of your entity and that enduring flame of which your youth and age, birth and death are but the inflections. (p. 106)

We leave it to the reader to determine how successful we were at the conclusion of this book, and we challenge our readers to build and improve on this work.

In subsequent chapters we present our results, describe their relevance, and explore possibilities for a (re)newed understanding of educational leadership.

Key Concepts

Heroic action. Educational leaders may not be heroes, but they should exhibit heroic action. In today's world of complex and interactive institutions, vision, courage, and persistence all play a role in catalyzing heroic actions on the part of educational leaders.

Leadership can be taught. Leaders learn how to lead. The consolidation of learning in formal texts or programs at universities, military academies, and the like is premised on the idea that becoming a leader can be taught. Unlocking the mysteries of leadership involves stepping inside the human heart for the heart has a logic all its own. School leaders' internal worlds can be probed and insights gained about their journeys even as they struggle with the difficulty of leading schools and making hard decisions.

Leadership journey. This journey involves school leaders undergoing a distinctive process of transformation that has identifiable phases. Thus, leadership results in new forms of seeing and learning.

Socially constructed process. Leadership is a culturally defined social process that is also transformational. Human beings learn how to induce others to follow them in the pursuit of desirable goals. Too often leaders' actions are only examined at the end of their transformation, giving the mistaken impression that their distinctiveness was present from birth.

Chapter Two

Witnessing Educational Leaders on the Mythic Journey

Behind this investigation was a quest to determine if leaders follow what Campbell describes as a universal mythology encompassing human development, life, and purpose. This is especially poignant for leaders, who must be able to inspire and motivate others. The challenge is that much more meaningful when the enterprise is quintessentially moral. Schools are not educating robots but future citizens of the world.

The research we did was actually an empirical assessment of the applicability of Campbell's explanation. We sought to test its parallelism as a compelling narrative with the power to help explain leadership in an imaginary realm. We saw ourselves as expanding the inquiry of leadership by moving into what sociologist Brown (1977) has coined "cognitive aesthetics" (p. 62), as shown in figure 2.1.

THE OVERLAPPING OF SCIENCE AND ART AND COGNITIVE AESTHETICS

Brown's (1977) notion is that art, like science, is rational. He argued that art and science both depend on experiences being formally organized into knowledge, making experience "intelligible." We are advancing "cognitive aesthetics" here to expand our inquiry into educational leadership.

Building on Brown (1977), we contend that educational leadership, like sociology, is "neither a natural science nor a fine art" (p. 3). As a system of coherence, when an "aesthetical view of rationality" (Brown, p. 3) is applied to the educational leadership field, it shares features of science *and* art.

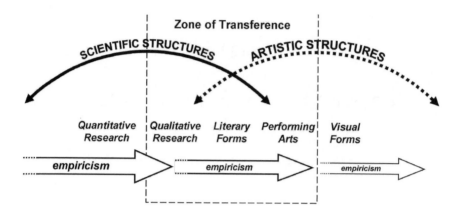

Figure 2.1.   The Overlapping of Science and Art and Cognitive Aesthetics

Cognitive aesthetics involves conducting research from a nexus different from those typically found in behavioral studies. Behaviorism itself is a lens that precludes us from seeing all the components of leadership because of assumptions about what constitutes a "scientific study" (English, 2002).

Science and scientific inquiry do not give us the full story. T. B. Greenfield similarly remarked over forty years ago in his controversial paper delivered in England that "the great issues that face us in education and administration cannot be understood from science alone" (see Greenfield & Ribbons, 1993, p. 225). Foster (1986), echoing the same perspective a dozen years later, observed, "The scientific study of leadership has essentially faltered, partly because the wrong phenomenon has been studied and partly because the functionalist paradigm that houses the studies has gone bankrupt" (p. 3).

Brown's (1977) notion of aesthetics in conducting research offered a promising perspective to rectify the shortcomings of past research. The promise of cognitive aesthetics means that a theatrical technique of showing not telling and momentarily becoming "objective" within this perspective is permitted—as in the case of viewing (and making meaning of) photographs of iconic people.

Generalizations from narratives using critical comments are encouraged. Events are allowed to show a panoramic view of things, presenting a narrative of simultaneity without being forced to adopt only one point of view or narrative for that matter.

This enhanced perspective allows for the inclusion of the emotional and subjective sides of leadership. The opening this creates can lead to the generation of data sources beyond economic rationality that dominates discussions about human decision-making today. Davis (2004) went so far as to refer to the popularization that fosters "the myth of the rational decision maker," which downplays, even eliminates, the importance of subjectivity in leadership (p. 622).

To be a decision-maker means using one's emotions and subjectivity. It also means to lead as a whole person whose perspective and life experience are not truncated and misleading to others. Barber's (1985) insight into U.S. presidential leadership corresponds with this concept:

> Every story of presidential decision-making is really two stories: an outer one in which a rational man calculates and an inner one in which an emotional man feels. The two are forever connected. Any real president is one whole man and his deeds reflect his wholeness. (p. 4)

EMPIRICISM, COGNITIVE AESTHETICS, AND THE ZONE OF TRANSFERENCE

The study of experience can be traced to empiricism and the idea that knowledge is based on sensory experience. Empiricism has a long history in the sciences and is part and parcel of both quantitative and qualitative research approaches. Its basic tenet is that "for one's beliefs to possess one or another truth-relevant merit, they must be related in one or another way to someone's experience" (Wolterstorff, 1999, p. 263).

Empiricism also emphasizes the role of evidence, in addition to experience, in the formation of ideas and knowledge (Wolterstorff, 1999). Observation employs five senses—sight, hearing, taste, smell, and touch. The senses are the physiological capacities that provide human beings with data about perception. In science, observation can also involve the reading of data using instruments.

The use of data most often occurs in the form of observation, as in when someone scrutinizes and reflects on photographic images. While empiricism has had its share of critics (e.g., Feyerabend, 1993; Popper, 1965), it remains a strong tradition in the sciences and, to a lesser extent, the arts.

In figure 2.2 we show that the realm of science has a strong referent in empiricism.

We advance the notion that cognitive aesthetics creates a space between science and art, which opens up intriguing possibilities for the continuing study of educational leadership. This figure shows the designation of this creative space where science and art overlap as the *zone of transference*. It is also a space where, as Brown (1977) posited, context and culture have defining roles in determining meaning.

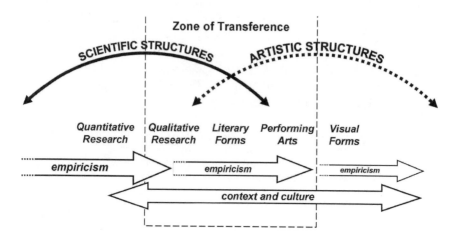

Figure 2.2.   Cognitive Aesthetics and the Zone of Transference

COGNITIVE AESTHETICS: THE ZONE OF TRANSFERENCE AND MAJOR EXPRESSIVE FORMS

In figure 2.3 we locate photography, painting, and sculpture as artistic structures. What is also emergent is that morality and the moral function of educational leadership become pronounced as themes within the zone of transference and artistic structures.

Samier, Bates, and Stanley (2006) persuasively argue that aesthetics is central to educational leadership: educational leaders are concerned about organizational culture, and its creation and implementation, which in turn is comprised of "language, symbolism, rituals, and ceremonies, focusing often on the creation of symbols of power, such as insignia" (p. 4). Just as leaders' worlds are infused with aesthetics relationally, organizationally, symbolically, and in other ways too, they use visual data, knowingly or unknowingly, to interpret cues in their environments.

THE USE OF VISUAL DATA

This study used *visual data* as prompts to explore the emotional and subjective sides of leadership. Such data have distinct advantages. We next describe three of them.

First, visual data are open-ended, especially compared with a survey. Surveys are restricted to Likert-scale responses that assign numerical value. The quantification of feelings and attitudes can sometimes be unreliable

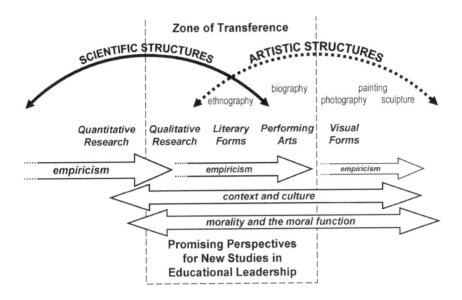

Figure 2.3.   Cognitive Aesthetics: The Zone of Transference and Major Expressive Forms for Studying Educational Leadership

because the researcher is relying on self-report, which may be inaccurate or difficult to map onto a numerical scale.

The Likert scale is based on the assumption that the psychological construct being measured is bipolar and unidirectional—it's linear, with the center point (e.g., the number 3 on a 5-point Likert scale) signifying neutrality, but this is not the same as ambivalence. In that regard, the Likert scale cannot measure ambivalence, because ambivalence and neutrality are not the same thing (Gardner, 1987).

The open-ended prompts we used with the photographs were broad in nature, allowing for ambivalence—the simultaneity of opposing attitudes or feelings, such as attraction and disgust toward something, in our study a powerful photograph, or uncertainty as to how to express one's thoughts and emotions—to be experienced. This way, the imagination was engaged.

Second, visual data appeal directly to the emotions. The role of emotions in leaders' lives, decision-making, and work have been underreported in research. Emotions are often erased in mechanistic accounts of decision-making anchored in rational choice theory (see Bolton & English, 2009, 2010a). Visual data go right to the heart.

Third, even though photographic data, especially of the human face, are culturally and linguistically bounded, there is still a universal quality to what they reveal. Support for this assertion comes from Ekman and Friesen

(2003). Their cross-cultural research established that there are six basic emotions—happiness, sadness, surprise, fear, anger, and disgust—shown on the human face.

Based on their 2003 study, Ekman and Friesen concluded that these emotions "were found by every investigator in the last thirty years who sought to determine the vocabulary of emotion terms associated with facial expression" (p. 22). The universal expressions were subsequently assembled by Ekman with another colleague (i.e., Ekman & Rosenberg, 2005) into the Facial Action Coding System (known as FACS) and given further credibility.

Empirical verification assures at least some collective recognition insofar as reading the human face.

PROBING THE INNER WORLD OF EDUCATIONAL LEADERS

To explore the inner world of educational leaders, we set out to determine the consciousness or intuition of a select number of practicing school leaders about their identity and work as a journey. We understood their identity construction to be a work in progress. To look at this, we took our participants through in a series of initiating phases (the calling) and culminating phases (e.g., recrossing) aligned with Campbell's model of the universal myth.

As indicated in chapter 1, we interviewed K–12 public school leaders and most interviews lasted an hour, with some going over. Interviews were digitally taped, and extensive notes were taken.

Each participant was shown three stacks, each containing eleven photographs or graphic designs. The photographs were taken from a variety of sources (books, newspapers, and magazines), and all were mounted on the same-sized backing. Only four (12 percent) of the thirty-three photographs did not feature the human face directly or visual images of humans partaking in a range of activities, from rug-weaving to a funeral.

Many people in the photographs had attained some degree of notoriety or fame. For example, there were full facials of Ingmar Bergman, Isaiah Berlin, Lennie Bruce, Michael Collins, Joseph Goebbels, Jimi Hendrix, Janis Joplin, Barbara Jordan, and Charles Lindberg.

Each participant was told:

> There are three stacks of photographs in front of you [all were face down]. I'm going to ask you some questions. After each question I would ask that you sort through each of the three stacks of photos/images and select the one that you think best answers the question. I will ask you to explain your selection. Then I will ask you to rank them 1, 2, or 3 in order of their ability to most fully capture your thoughts. Is that clear? Before I ask you any questions, turn the

stacks over and go through the photos/images to acquaint yourself with them. When you are ready for the first question, let us know.

These are the five questions in the order that they were asked.

1. Select the photos/images in each of the three stacks that in your view best represent the "human condition" in this world. Explain your choices.
2. Now select the photos/images in each of the three stacks that best represent the trials in life that each human must face. Explain your choices.
3. Next select the photos/images that best show the concept of human transformation or change. Explain your choices.
4. Now select the photos/images that best show a human being crossing an important threshold in life. Explain your choices.
5. Finally, select the photos/images that best illustrate leadership. Explain your choices.

The participants (school leaders) reacted to the images, making such comments as, "Wow, that is a powerful image that I can't quite place in time, but I feel a stirring just looking at it" and "That funeral scene makes me think instantaneously of death and of how short life really is."

There were obviously no "right" answers, and we gave no clues to prompt the thinking process or reactions beyond the initial questions. Most were initially able to sort with some definitiveness until they narrowed their choices; then they took time to make a final selection—conspicuously reflective about this task!—and rank their top three, one from each pile, in order of their selection.

The most interesting aspect of the interviews was the commentaries they spontaneously produced. Participants explained the reasons for their selections. Within the narratives they told, they explained their choices using their own experiences, conflicts, or issues, and they reflected on personal and/or professional ethical dilemmas that the images produced.

Some of the photographs touch human sentiment, a fact that was reinforced when participants struggled with their emotions, in at least one instance being moved to tears. The images of a world from the past and distant past tugged at their current worlds and presented selves. In their expressions and utterances, we witnessed temporal cross-overs and collapses in time. We observed personal connection in a line of expression, in the glint of an eye, and in the single movement of a hand.

Literary photographer Sontag (1977) summarized this phenomenon:

> Photography is the paradigm of an inherently equivocal connection between
> self and world—its version of the ideology of realism sometimes dictating an
> effacement of the self in relation to the world, sometimes authorizing an ag-
> gressive relation to the world which celebrates the self. (p. 123)

Photography elicits a connection between people's inner and outer worlds.

Because it is not a snapshot of reality, a person can feel effaced by a particular photo—when a photograph excludes them—or celebrated—when a photo honors them or what they represent. Other possibilities that speak to the self-world connection include feeling overwhelmed, attracted, enraged, or repulsed.

SUBJECTIVITY/OBJECTIVITY/SUBJECTIVITY PARADOX

As the research project continued, we became aware of the *subjectivity/ objectivity paradox*. This paradox lies in the fact that a photographer made a subjective decision to take a picture of someone or something, but the camera simply accepted light rays as they were reflected in its mechanism, an objective representation—a fact, if you will. But the resulting photograph must be interpreted by a viewer within his or her own subjectivity.

From this vantage point, our respondents' narratives did not involve an objective reality, but rather a personal reading of a topographical reality. The interaction with a photograph was merely a prompt for that individual's reality (inner world). Therefore, every photograph always has two viewings simultaneously.

The first is the view of the photographer.

And the second is the person who sees the photograph.

This is the same dilemma that Campbell (1972/1993) described as the *mystical function* of a living mythology, a kind of awakening that produces

> a sense of awe and gratitude in relation to the mystery dimension of the
> universe, not so that he lives in fear of it, but so that he recognizes that he
> participates in it, since the mystery of being is the mystery of his own deep
> being as well. (pp. 214–215)

Campbell is saying that the universe is one with the person living in it. One of the purposes of mythology is to dissolve the binary between subjectivity and objectivity and the illusion of separation in our minds. The use of visual images in our research performed the same function—to collapse the subjective (inner) and objective (outer) worlds.

Human Condition—Walking along a River

Participants were first asked "to select the photos/images that best represent-ed the human condition. The three stacks were color coded: one pink, one yellow, and the last blue." When computing frequency of selection, an image earned a "1" if it was selected first, second, or third.

The reason is that as researchers we made no assumptions that any rank-ing was represented on a ratio interval scale (think percentiles on a standard-ized test); rather, it was ordinal only (like arranging people in a room by height or weight). This meant that for a person who ranked a photo second, the interval was not necessarily the same from two to one as from two to three.

The results of the selection were interesting in that over half of the re-spondents selected a photograph of African Americans in a group walking with a revered figure along a river together. The mood is clearly reverential toward this figure, and the expressions of happiness are celebratory.

The designation of this image as the most frequently selected to represent "the human condition" parallels Campbell's notion of a journey in a cycle of life. The river connotes the flow of water and events. Walking alongside a waterway conjures associative images with, or feelings of, time and motion, as well as power.

It turns out the photograph was of George Baker (1879–1965) of Rock-ville, Maryland, also known as "Father Devine" to thousands of followers in the 1920s and 1930s. An African American, he began as a Baltimore garden-er and travelling Baptist preacher. Determined, he wanted to bring his fol-lowers together and live under one roof. They ran an employment agency for domestics and gardeners in what was called "the Peace Mission Movement."

The living arrangement brought together African Americans who enjoyed spiritual communion and the message of freedom for Black peoples. Later the movement was joined by wealthy White people who pooled funds and invested in hotels, restaurants, and other businesses using Father Devine's profits. There is no evidence he ever profited from any of the funds.

Father Devine preached a strong self-help doctrine where drugs and alco-hol were not permitted. Followers had to clean up and get a job. Father Devine's Kingdom on Earth was integrated at a time when such things were indeed very rare. Later a claim was advanced that the Peace Mission fed more New Yorkers during the Great Depression than all of the city's other relief houses. Gates and West (2000) confirmed that "Father Devine's move-ment was a unique phenomenon in black life, led by a fascinating figure with his mind set, in part, on black freedom" (p. 122).

One of the functions of a living mythology is the mystical condition we have already spoken about, the sense that one is in harmony with the uni-verse. Another function of a living mythology is "to validate, support and imprint the norms of a given, specific moral order, that namely, of the society in which the individual is to live" (Campbell, 1972/1993, p. 215). This second function is more about continuing norms and customs.

Several sources of happiness are shown in the photo of Father Devine walking along the river with his followers, both Black and White people. The type of happiness is not registered as a smiling face. Instead, it is an emotion Shweder (1994) called "affiliated," something felt and expressed in others' company. According to Ekman and Friesen (2003), this type of happiness

> involves the self-concept. Something happens that enhances your view of yourself, something that affirms or further elaborates a favorable self-concept. . . . If someone tells you that you have done a good job at something, you feel happy. Praise, friendship, the esteem of others is rewarding and makes you feel happy. It is not the kind of happiness in which you usually will burst out laughing. It is a more contented, smiling happiness. (p. 101)

The respondents who selected this photograph made such remarks as "It signifies forward progress, a new era and unity" and

> It resonates a centuries-old struggle for individual and collective freedom. . . . This picture seems to intimate their celebrating collectively. It's almost like a march. That to me is the greatest example of triumph. . . . People are smiling in the picture. Multi-generations represented. There is a man walking in the front. He might be a minister.

Someone else commented, "We are on a journey. . . . Life is about discovery, about creating who we are. It should be about discovering our gifts." The responses clearly showed the extent to which the school leaders read into these visual images their own interpretations, in essence validating the notion that a photograph always has two viewers or simultaneous views.

Three other photographs were selected by at least a third of our interviewees each time. These were all close-up images of pensive or serious women. One was a full-face shot of a woman staring directly at the viewer. The emotion verged on sadness without displaying sadness.

A second photo has been called "the most reproduced image in the history of photography and is known to many people who could not name its author" (Wells, 2005, p. 37). It was taken in 1936 by Dorothea Lange and has been called *Migrant Mother*. We comment on this in more detail in chapter 3 when we consider the "meaning" of photographs.

The comments from participants about the second photo advanced such interpretations as human concern and worry, as in: "She is concerned about what is going on. It may not have happened yet. She is the worry figure." Worry was mythologized.

As for the close-up of the woman weaver, "As human beings today we are trying to figure out a lot of different puzzles. The loom and weave represent the fabric of life." Life is a puzzle. The viewer is a leader is a weaver confronted and challenged by puzzles. The selection of human faces in a serious mode peering into space is another conveyance of the human condition. In none of the photographs could it be said that an image was conveyed of a person in total control of life.

Trials in Life

School leaders were next asked to select photos regarding trials in life. Two photographs were chosen by four participants. The first was of a funeral in the Andes with South American peasants. The crude casket is open, the person's face is covered, and a large wooden cross lies on the body. Spectators are standing around, some holding their hats. A somber scene.

While quietly peering at this pictorial display, one leader moved from a surface reading to an increasingly interpretive one about the meaning and purpose of life—in just moments while transported in time, saying,

> It appears to be a funeral. There is a casket and a cross. Latino families mourning a loss. Challenges are a loss. The death of a parent. It's the loss of innocence. Loss of reality and the loss of hope. The biggest things we deal with, knowing that loss is a part of life. Lives on earth are temporal. It's an awakening to the fact we have limited time and it's important to find meaning and purpose in what this life is all about.

Another remarked, "It's about the struggles we have in life. We're all going to be buried someday. We need to make things better for kids. It's a short amount of time that we're here."

Still another leader said that the photograph captures communal grief by depicting the "casket of a small child being mourned." Elaborating on its meaning and the human tragedy inherent in the loss of the child, he remarked,

> Death happens to all of us. Her life was cut short and so her potential cannot be played out. There's no chance to fall in love. The casket is symbolic—it's the choices we make which might derail a career yet something can happen to cut our promise short; someone in this crowd [in the photo] has a deep connection.

While there was loss transmitted for the beloved in the "crowd," the child's own journey was also referenced as a type of loss. The loss seemed to be more about the fact that the deceased would never have the experience to live out her potential, as in to have a career, or to fall in love. The image of the "crowd" registered one beloved's emotive connection in particular. Perhaps some of the leaders were thinking about the death as a cross to bear, maybe even possibly transcend, for the survivors on their journey of life.

Migrant Mother was the second photo selected by four other participants, and it was also chosen to describe the human condition. Dorothea Lange's *Migrant Mother* is an example of photographs used in this research that resemble great poetry and *are* poetic. Evocative, the images have potentially countless layers of meaning, which the viewers identified in different ways. Like poetry, photographs are viewed within cultural conditions that change over time and yet have a powerful immediacy, such as around the universal experience of death and loss.

Photographs also tap into Goleman's (1998) perspective on emotional intelligence, which he defined as "the capacity for recognizing our own feelings and those of others, for motivating ourselves, and for managing emotions well in ourselves and in our relationships" (p. 317).

While we did not measure "emotional intelligence" among our respondents, nearly all exhibited the capacity for understanding human feelings and perceptions with little more to work from than photographs. We did not witness any examples of mismanaged emotions but then we had not put energy toward this being a potential concern. We did "regulate" our own emotions by listening closely to the comments and by responding only in ways consistent with our protocol and the prompts.

Human Triumph

Human triumph matched the "confronting reality" and "atonement" aspects of Campbell's leadership journey. The overwhelming choice (64 percent) of the respondents for this stage in the leadership journey was the photo of Father Devine with his followers on the river walk. A typical comment was "It looks like a group of people who are happy being together. They've accomplished some sort of victory."

The fact that photographs can carry many meanings and messages should be rather obvious, but at the personal level photographs can have particular meanings that are highly charged. They can be very powerful and evince strong emotions and associations with life experiences.

Our intention for this entire study was to arrive at some understanding of the hidden meanings of the events in Campbell's leadership journey narrative. Like Campbell, we used an approach Henley (1998) considered "hermeneutical/interpretative," one "in which society is conceived as a text or language whose meaning must be explicated by an analyst who has achieved 'communicative competence' in the relevant cultural norms and practices" (p. 44).

The school leaders we interviewed had achieved such cultural competence. One of the functions of a school in any society is the transmission of culture and specific cultural norms. That school leaders were practiced in those norms was revealed through our study.

We also witnessed in the responses of the leaders what Barthes (1980) observed, that the "essence" of a photograph can be separated into two parts: the "stadium" and the "punctum."

The former term refers to that part of a photograph that is familiar to everyone functioning in a similar cultural code, and it is largely an aesthetic or informational response.

The punctum, by contrast, is a photograph with shock value that triggers an emotional response, setting off a flow of personal memories and associations, perhaps unconsciously.

Both levels were present in the photographs employed in this study.

Human Transformation

Human transformation is called the "apotheosis" in Campbell's universal journey narrative. Campbell (as cited in Larsen & Larsen, 1991) himself framed it as when "one is transparent to the transcendent" (p. 547), which meant following "atonement": Where there is a unification for the traveler comes the ultimate insight. One is forever changed or at least significantly transformed as result.

Four photographs tied for the most responses to this prompt. The first was a photograph of a smiling young woman who is pushing up her left brow with her finger. She is conveying that she is onto something and is pleased about it. Her expression is anchored to self-concept, "something that affirms or further elaborates a favorable self-concept" (Ekman & Friesen, 2003, p. 101).

The next photograph was of Barbara Jordan. In it, she is raising her hand to make a point in a debate. Jordan was the first African American since 1883 to serve in the Texas Senate. In 1972 she became the first Black woman elected to Congress from the South. A former lawyer, she was recognized as an expert on the U.S. Constitution. The picture shows her confidence and communicates human transformation.

Once Jordan was asked if she was nervous being not only a woman but also a Black woman in a legislature filled with males perceived to be sexist and racist, to which she replied, "You must understand, I have a tremendous amount of faith in my own capacity. I know how to read and write and think, so I have no fear" (as cited in Gates & West, 2000, p. 300). Jordan had held up a mirror to the initiator of this interchange whose assumptions were ill-placed about her.

Referring to Jordan, one respondent said, "This is someone who is thinking change is necessary. We can't continue to do things the old way." Indeed, Jordan's legislative record shows she pushed for fair employment practices and worked for training and education programs for people with disabilities. She crafted laws to improve workman's compensation, one of which led to the founding of the Texas First Employment Practices Commission.

The third photograph is a single face showing the six basic emotions from Ekman and Friesen's (2003) research. One of the school leaders remarked, "This depicts the schizophrenia of leadership, the different faces you wear. What is true of you? What is your façade?" Another leader commented, "One person's different faces, attitudes, expressions—we all have different faces every day."

The last selection was a photograph of Nazi soldier formations marching through Munich, though for most of the school leaders it appeared to be just formations of soldiers marching. They were unfamiliar with the historical context represented in the image. One respondent noted, "These are people who are willing to accept an ideology that was very foreign." Someone else commented, "You can see that change was occurring in the course of how people thought about other people." About leadership, an insight shared was, "How powerful we can be to influence other people and how if you get it right with leadership you can influence change."

Indeed, how powerful leaders can be to influence other people and how if they get it right with leadership they can influence change. The leaders did identify the marching soldiers as a force of authority that was having an impact on the behavior and perceptions of the onlookers, the citizens of a place. They recognized that what they were looking at was not merely soldiers marching, as in a parade, but soldiers having an influence in some way. With very few contextual clues, participants picked up on how influential leadership can be and that leaders can influence change, presumably in a positive or negative direction.

About the march in the Bavarian city of Munich, Daniel Goldhagen (1996), professor of government and social sciences at Harvard University, describes the Beer Hall *putsch* in 1923. Adolf Hitler and the Nazi Party had led a coalition group in this march, aiming to seize control and overthrow the German federal government. They wanted to put in place a new government to oversee the creation of a Greater German Reich, unified around citizenship based on race.

Although the putsch failed, resulting in the prosecution of Hitler and others by Bavarian authorities in an act of independence, the German leaders succeeded by absorbing their failure into the mythos of Hitler and the Nazis' rise to power. They ultimately reframed Hitler's march as a heroic effort, propagandizing that it played a part in the courageous actions of a visionary leader to save the nation (Goldhagen, 1996).

Heroic actions can be falsifications of truth. They can arise out of the oppression of people and they can be used to advance a systematic program to assassinate people, in this case to annihilate the Jews in the course of war.

The call to peacemaking can be used as a means to propagate lies, to negatively influence people, and to create a dictatorship that positions one person and one party to be in control of a nation. An associated emotion is fear.

We personally know of educational leaders who have been called "dictator" behind their backs by followers who suffer targeting campaigns by their superiors to gain absolute power and to subordinate all subjects. This is the antithesis of the kind of followship that fosters peacemaking in the nation's public schools and schools of education. Leaders need to get it right with leadership and leave fear-mongering (i.e., the use of fear by dictators to influence people's opinions and actions toward some specific end) to military dictatorships of the past.

Crossing Back

In Campbell's leadership journey, after the experience of apotheosis the individual must cross back over the threshold and return to humankind. The expectation at this point is to teach others the lessons learned and thereby impart wisdom. This part of the educative journey can be rewarding, illuminating, or even traumatic for some.

The photographs selected by our participants were also chosen for other aspects of the leadership journey. These included Dorothea Lange's *Migrant Mother*—a pensive woman whose facial expression is lined with worry—and the surprising selection of social commentator (comedian) Lennie Bruce, who is giving the viewer the finger. This is perhaps the most obscene gesture within Anglo-Saxon culture. Its usage can be traced back to ancient Roman times (see Morris, Collett, Marsh, & O'Shaughnessy, 1979). (In the British Isles it is made with two fingers instead of one.)

The gesture is intended to be offensive under any circumstances, and in this case it is a sign of defiance. One respondent said intriguingly of the image, "You reach the point where you've had enough. It doesn't matter." The response was nonjudgmental about the gesture. Simpatico?

Leadership

The last query put to our respondents was to identify the visual images that best represented the nature of leadership. Five of the eleven school leaders decided on the photograph of famed film director Ingmar Bergman (1990) "framing" a shot on location. By *framing* we mean he is holding up both hands and forming a square to determine what the camera will see when shooting begins for a scene. That they selected this photograph more frequently than the others is significant.

The school leaders' comments were informative: "This person is framing. A leader needs to have a framework. A leader has to make sense of the problem." Someone remarked,

> You've got to have vision. You have to see the big picture and be willing to look ahead to what you see things to be. You have to get people to help the vision become a reality. And then become part of that vision. Leaders have to let people become part of that.

Yet another said,

> You're looking at the world through a lens—that is what leadership is about. The lens might be social justice, school edicts from the state, a view of the whole child, or a parental viewpoint. There are lots of different lenses for leading schools and districts, and questions that need to be asked.

FRAMING AS THE ESSENCE OF LEADERSHIP

The framing visual was highly evocative. Framing provides cognitive and emotional maps in which humans can come together and focus on communal work. Leaders help define the continuities and ruptures in the work of an organization. They bring meaning and stability to the organization and create workspaces that enable people's narratives to be lived and expressed, thereby making "the unexpected expectable, hence manageable" (Robinson, 1981, p. 60).

In Karl Weick's (1995) classic *Sensemaking in Organizations*, *sensemaking* is defined as stimuli that are placed into a framework of some kind. Our research did just that—we loosely organized stimuli taking the form of photographic images and for this purpose we used Campbell's journey framework. In this way, while we conceived of a frame for the photos, the leaders who spoke to them spontaneously created their own frames as meaning-makers. Our frames and their frames coalesced around the journey motif and its phases.

A frame of reference is crucial for leading schools and, as Weick makes clear, critical when something interrupts the normal flow of events. He writes,

> To understand sensemaking is also to understand how people cope with interruptions. The joint influence of expectations and interruptions suggests that sensemaking will be more or less of an issue in organizations, depending on the adequacy of the scripts, routines, and recipes already in place. (p. 5)

As Weick states, frames include scripts and routines that provide direction and support for coping.

Sensemaking involves approaching knowledge in a creative, adaptive way. Thus, as Louis (2006) writes, knowledge is "not an objective 'thing' to be used in the way we use a tool to achieve a clear and fixed purpose" (p. 7). Accordingly, what we are aspiring to produce in an ongoing way as leaders is "a set of cognitive understandings that are changed and developed during the process of applying them" (Louis, p. 7).

From this perspective, leadership involves close attention to the social process in using knowledge (Louis, 2006). Out of sheer necessity and survival, then, sensemaking is a process in which meaning is produced, no matter how complex or ambiguous the information may be. Not just ambiguous but also perplexing, we decided to use visual data as our information source.

The images we had selected registered emotions on the human face. The photographs forced an openness on the part of the viewer and engagement to interpret and assess meaning. All the participants moved from one interpretative act to another. Each made connections and revisited meanings, becoming more selective with their photographic selections and more reflective.

With very little prompting, respondents reflected on their own lives and lived experiences, using their imaginations to shape cognitive understandings. For example, whether or not they had personally suffered the loss of a child, they identified not only with this loss but also with the accompanying loss for the loved one and the deceased, a child whose life journey was shockingly abandoned—unlived. They had the opportunity to exercise their imaginations while advancing cognitive understandings.

This is exactly the kind of situation required of educational leaders in schools as they confront "reality" every day. March and Olsen (1976) capture this predicament:

> Most of what we believe we know about elements within organizational choice situations, as well as the events themselves, reflects an interpretation of events by organizational actors and observers. Those interpretations are generated within the organization in the face of considerable perceptual ambiguity. (p. 19)

"Perceptual ambiguity" forces the need for interpretation—mandates come and go, leaders come and go, and nothing remains fixed or stable. One person's view of an event or another person is different from someone else's, and both are subject to change. Experiential states, motivational states, and emotional states all influence perception.

Consider how a hiring process and search committees tend to work: Ambiguity or lack of information about the candidate leads to a greater need for facts. References are contacted for their "read" of the individual who is being judged. The references may have very different, even contradictory, things to say, which makes the fact-finding mission seem elusive. Much needs to be inferred about candidates and about what others have to say about them, which perpetuates ambiguity to a greater degree than specificity. In such scenarios and in daily living, we attempt to create a stable picture of people in a context of perpetual ambiguity where there are many moving parts. Yet we fixate on facts.

Following the emphasis placed on human interpretation in organizations by March and Olsen (1976), organizational philosopher James March (1984) expanded his thinking, commenting that "organizational life is as much about interpretation, intellect, metaphors of theory, and fitting our history into an understanding of life as it is about decisions and coping with the environment" (p. 18).

Being able to wisely interpret people's character, intentions, and actions, as well as situations and events, is key as a leader, not only making decisions and coping. Experiential learning as a leader and learning from experience are also essential to March's (1984) organizational tenets.

What we see in the results of our work thus far is that school leaders interpret their inner and outer worlds, and they create frameworks to make sense of stimuli they encounter. They do it every day in their work lives. When confronted with a scenario involving a larger set of stimuli, such as life, death, and loss, they resort to familiar cultural frameworks that bring discrepant events into a narrative that goes beyond schooling and that may entail life, death, or loss.

ABOUT OUR RESPONDENTS' WORLDS

The school leaders responded to powerful images and the world of possibilities each one conveyed to them. We experienced the emotional levels of their involvement in making meaning of selected photographs. Their responses and our own experiences stimulated us to reflect on our own viewpoints, as next expressed.

We do not claim that the responses of our school leaders to emotional and ambiguous visual stimuli "prove" that they were unconsciously following Campbell's leadership journey. Like Popper (1968), we hold that no one can ever "prove" a theory. Rather, it is only possible to *disprove* a theory. It is the case that our work does not refute Campbell's framework of the universal mythological narrative journey.

Rather, we see our respondents' oral tellings about the photographic visuals as a parallel form of Campbell's journey, with many connections. Some of these connections, which are open-ended interpretations, have been explained by us and others left to the reader's own construction. That human life consists of an awareness of things behind symbols, signs, and metaphors—and that it involves trials of all sorts, surprises, and intuitive sparks—

generates a cognitive mapping. This mapping allows the interpreter to formulate understandings of our encounters along the way.

Campbell's framework involved sensemaking about what on the surface appeared to be a thousand different stories and characters with plot twists and surprises. Initially these appeared to have little in common, yet Campbell's cognitive map enabled us to see patterns among them as well as to make "sense" of them in a way that was reassuring.

Don't we tend to seek comfort in our sometimes baffling and confusing worlds? Campbell's (1972/1993) leadership journey narrative fulfills the fourth function of living mythology, which is "to guide [one], stage by stage, in health, strength, and harmony of spirit," through the "course of a useful life" (p. 215).

In our respondents' choices of photographs and explanations we saw similar archetypes identified across time and cultures by Campbell. We sensed the same rhythms in the descriptions of unfamiliar stimuli the school leaders provided. We saw them struggle with the ambiguity and complexity inherent in sensemaking, as well as with their own emotions. They were given very little instruction. They had no mandate to follow, and they had no one else to turn to for clues or explanation, support or guidance.

We really believe that we saw hearts move, not just emotions triggered and reasons sought after. We were reminded of what Mahatma Gandhi (as cited in Iyer, 1973/2000) once said: "If you want something really important to be done, you must not merely satisfy the reason, you must move the heart also" (p. 287). Archetypes were suggestively present in the participants' words. We witnessed framing and saw a common face of humanity emerge from the school leaders' discourse.

In that space with us, the leaders were not locked into mental prisons of functional thinking and managerial efficiency. The associations they made and the stories they told, with very little prompting and almost no context, were artful. They shared in ways that made them seem humane and sensitive. Not only that, they came across as thoughtful about uses of power and aware of values that serve citizens—all reflective of leaders and other actors who conduct themselves as artists or artfully (English, 2008b; Mullen, 1999). In these ways, the leaders revealed artistry in leadership, making evocative connections between their inner and outer selves, and their personal identities and historical identities.

The importance of revealing this connectivity between self and others is underscored by KetsdeVries (1993), who remarked trenchantly, "One of a leader's most important roles is to be aware of and to accommodate the emotional needs of subordinates" (p. 35).

Key Concepts

A living mythology. This refers to the notion that certain narratives offer a vibrant, relevant mythic framework for daily living. These enable people to come to a sense of understanding of the universe and their own place within it and of the times and norms of a given social and cultural order (Campbell, 1972/1993).

Cognitive aesthetics. This is a perspective regarding research conducted on educational administration and/or leadership in which the emotional side of decision-making is included (based on the work of Brown, 1977).

Framing. Perhaps the most important function of leaders within an organization is to provide a frame of reference for making meaning of disruptive or discrepant events. Weick (1995) underscores the importance of using narratives for framing because "people think narratively rather than argumentatively or paradigmatically" (p. 127). Leaders produce framing when they tell stories.

Subjectivity/objectivity paradox. A paradox is a statement that is simultaneously true and false. In this respect, visual data such as photographs are both subjective and objective. A photographer takes a picture (subjective); the picture is recorded mechanically (objective) and is then interpreted by a viewer (subjective). Making meaning of such data is highly personal, and the more ambiguous the images, the more the viewer inserts personal life experiences into an interpretation (see Sontag, 1977).

Visual data. Such data are located in cinematic film, television, maps, drawings, still photography, and various forms of artistic representation. They are highly interpretative and often involve cross-cultural understanding. One branch of such study is visual anthropology (Banks, 2001).

Zone of transference. This is a conceptual space where science and art overlap and where promising new perspectives for studying and researching educational leadership may be located (as identified in English, 2008a).

Chapter Three

Seeing, Believing, and Constructing Meaning

In this chapter we present the unique nature of photographic data and its connection to storytelling for leaders and leadership. Specifically, we address the data we collected and aspects of visual data within contexts of interpretation. Eighty-eight percent of the photographs featured the human face or a full human figure. Some—like Lennie Bruce, Jimi Hendrix, Janis Joplin, Barbara Jordan, and Charles Lindberg—were famous Americans. Others, such as Ingmar Bergman, Isaiah Berlin, and Michael Collins, were international personalities.

There are two major perspectives on how to read—or make sense of—a photograph. The first centers on whether the image is based on reality. The second involves "the interpretation of the image by focusing upon the reading, rather than the taking, of photographic representations" (Wells, 2005, p. 24).

The tradition of viewing photographs has evolved since the first portraits of people appeared in France in 1839. Louis-Jacques-Mandé Daguerre was recognized for his invention of the daguerreotype process of photography. It was the first practicable photographic process and a precursor to the camera. Called at the time "Daguerrotypes," portrait photography became hugely popular in the 1850s and 1860s (Trachtenberg, 2007).

What a photographic portrait "meant" in the nineteenth and early twentieth century into the twenty-first century has changed. In earlier times it was thought that portraits needed to reveal the inner essence of the human subject photographed. These so-called inner truths could be discerned because the face was a mirror of the soul, or so it was believed. The job of a great photographer was to reveal the subject's inner truths so viewers could perceive them.

This tradition of photography survived well into the twentieth century but is now passé. Instead Vicki Goldberg (1987), the biographer of famous photographer Margaret Bourke-White, said of her work, "Her best pictures are brilliantly symbolic, summary, telegraphic: they remain to teach us, and sometimes to rebuke us" (p. 364).

Roland Barthes (1977), French literary theorist/philosopher, also observed that photography is a powerful medium not because of its ability to reveal but rather its capacity to be "pensive"—"it thinks." The point is that a photograph is no longer a one-dimensional rendering of a single truth; rather, photographs are multilayered and multi-perspectival. They serve to teach and provoke viewers.

The cultural tradition of viewing a photograph today, and the one behind the methods of this study, revolves around *aporia* (Derrida, 1993). Photographs possess a kind of indeterminacy, a movement that is shifting, bound only within the borders of what is included within it at the moment it is taken.

Viewers today understand the impermanency of what has been captured in a photograph. Berger (1972) noted the same phenomenon: "It is seeing which establishes our place in the surrounding world; while we explain that world with words . . . the relationship between what we see and what we know is never settled" (p. 7). The world cannot be explained with words alone.

There was no presupposition that the "reality" of a photograph is independent of either the photographer or the viewer. The photographer is working simultaneously at composition, finding the proper angle and determining what is in or out of the picture. Once captured, the image is frozen in time.

Price (1994) contends that the meaning of a photographic image is determined by the words in which it is embedded and the use to which it is put. Price indicates that "there is no single meaning for a photograph, but rather an emergent meaning, within which the subject-matter of the image is but one element" (p. 28).

This is what French philosopher Jacques Derrida (1993) meant when he described *aporia* as moving between two languages. Expressions in one language are not always precisely translatable in another. The space between two languages is an aporia. This can also be said of photographs. Because the exact meaning of a photograph is untranslatable, one must create meaning.

The value of a photograph is the context or story in which it is embedded. Take, for example, a scrapbook of family snapshots. To make sense of such photographs, they must be accompanied by stories about the flow of events in which the snapshots were anchored. These images exemplify social construction—meaning-making by individuals about the world and understandings shared by others—and contain messages and a kind of exhibition code.

Code refers not only to the composition of the photograph but also to "the pattern of social habits and conventions responsible for what people do in snapshots" (Chalfen, 2001, p. 227). Such homemade snapshots are a form of world-making "that is repeated and duplicated with remarkable consistency" (p. 230). Human perception is then patterned, or follows patterns.

While photographs were the prompts (surface data) for our study, the deeper data were the stories sparked for the respondents. Mythologically speaking, the data were Janus like—they contained two faces: one the image, the other the story.

A Her/story of the *Migrant Mother* Photograph

Migrant Mother by Dorothea Lange has been called "one of the world's greatest news photographs" (Wells, 2005, p. 37). It has moved from being just a photograph to becoming an icon, the subject of magazine covers and even a U.S. postage stamp (see figure 3.1).

The story behind *Migrant Mother* explains its power. Lange had already spent the day photographing for the Farm Security Administration. Near the evening she stopped to investigate a group of workers picking peas. The woman in the photograph, later identified as Florence Thompson, was seated in a makeshift tent with her children.

Lange recounted that she did not ask Thompson's name, but she did get her age (thirty-two). Thompson told Lange that her family had been subsisting on frozen vegetables from the fields and birds that one of her children killed. She had sold the tires from her car to buy food for her family. While the photograph made Thompson famous, she later confessed that she never earned a penny from it.

When a photograph is considered "authentic," it is understood to be of the scene or what actually appeared. Retouching and other tricks of the trade should not be used. However, Lange the photographer later admitted that just as she was taking the photo of Thompson, a hand had reached out to pull back the tent flap. Her camera caught a thumb, which she did later retouch out. Critics have disapproved this action, but such criticism is only valid if one judges a photograph on the basis of whether it is true to "reality," that is, untouched.

However, if a photograph is not judged by how well it corresponds to "reality," then there is another way to appraise it. It involves interpretation of what the image "represents." For example, *Migrant Mother* could be a symbol of politics and ideology at work.

Or the photograph could be used to provoke a discussion on class, race, and gender. Consider that Lange's photograph "was premised on the assertion that the victims of the Depression [like Thompson] were to be judged as the deserving poor"; the focus on "individual misfortune" meant that "sys-

Figure 3.1. Migrant Mother

tematic failure in the political, economic, and social spheres" was not being examined, which is the deeper issue (Solomon-Godeau, 1991, p. 179).

Another perspective on *Migrant Mother* revolves around gender. The photo evokes strong images of the maternal aspects of womanhood, in which the viewer sees

> the way the image of a damaged femininity came to symbolize the crisis of community for the American public. Anxious and in obvious poverty, the woman holds on to her two children, suggesting the power of material values to overcome the most dire of circumstances. Here is a woman who has lost everything, yet heroically, stoically keeps her family together. (Roberts, 1998, p. 85)

From this perspective, heroic action by a woman, who is a strong maternal figure, is being conveyed in photographic terms.

As researchers, we attach no "final" meaning to any of the images used in the study. Presenting the photos was not about trying to convey or represent "the truth" but rather to provide each viewer/respondent/storyteller with the opportunity to spontaneously speak of individual associations with powerful concepts. In our study these constituted the human condition, trials in life, human triumph, human transformation, human crossing, and leadership.

Total Configuration Concept

Consider how we take in environments and navigate them, observing how one thing is related to another and, without even thinking about it, having a "total picture" from which to operate. Along these lines, management guru Peter Drucker (1974) wrote, "Perception, we know, is not logic. It is experience. This means, in the first place, that one always perceives a configuration. One cannot perceive single specifics. They are always part of a total picture" (p. 483).

Drucker also spoke of *total configuration* as "the silent language" by which a person's gestures, tone of voice, and work environment "cannot be dissociated from spoken language. In fact, without them the spoken word has no meaning and cannot communicate" (p. 483). From this perspective, connections to culture and social commitments play a vital role in the total picture perceived.

Campbell found a unique "total picture" and introduced an aesthetic referred to as "the art of reading myths" (Larsen & Larsen, 1991, p. 334). Humans make sense of their world with such "total pictures," which are usually embodied in the stories they tell. Leadership is about telling stories because this is what humans do, circulate narratives. It is the way people make sense of their experiences and communicate meaning more fully to others.

Howard Gardner's (1995) study of leaders concludes that stories matter in a leader's influence: "The ultimate impact of the leader depends most significantly on the particular story that he or she relates or embodies, and the receptions to that story on the part of audiences (or collaborators or followers)" (p. 14).

This American psychologist states that because audiences also have stories about their experiences, the mission of the leader in competing for followers is to connect with stakeholders through telling stories. Gardner (1995) explains that together leaders and followers

> have embarked on a journey in pursuit of certain goals, and along the way and into the future, they can expect to encounter certain obstacles or resistances that must be overcome. Leaders and audiences traffic in many stories, but the most basic story has to do with issues of identity. (p. 14)

As you can see, Gardner's explanation of how stories interact with one another parallels Campbell's idea of the universal leadership journey. Identity formation and development are an essential part of storytelling. Storytelling using the broad brush strokes of the journey motif from initiation to departure to return gives a total picture view of our lives.

The Leader, the Story, and the "Fit"

When a leader truly connects with an audience, it becomes a matter of *fit*. At that moment in time the experiences and explanations of life being shared by the leader fit with the largest number of followers. One of the most potent examples of "fit" was the legendary union activist Mother Jones, a.k.a. Mary Harris (1837–1930), a fiery activist who spoke to coal and gold miners in a way no one else could.

A miner remembered Mother Jones, in her high-pitched Irish brogue: She "could permeate a group of strikers with more fight than could any living human being. She fired them with enthusiasm . . . burned them with criticism, then cried with them. . . . The miners loved, worshipped, and adored her" (Gorn, 2001b, p. 181).

Mother Jones led by example when she told her followers on presenting a petition to the Governor of Colorado,

> Take this document to the Governor's office, present it to him yourselves and don't go on your knees: we have no kings in America. Stand erect on both feet with your head erect as citizens of this country and don't say "Your honor," very few have honor. They don't know what it is. (as cited in Gorn, 2001b, p. 203)

In a thirty-year odyssey for the miners' unions, Mother Jones became a powerhouse figure in America (Gorn, 2001b). According to biographer Elliott Gorn (2001b),

The way Mother Jones lived her life was breathtaking. She tailored her appearance to match every sentimental notion about mothers. Then she subverted the very idea of genteel womanhood on which such stereotypes were based with her vituperative, profane, electric speeches. Women—especially old women—were not supposed to have opinions about politics and economics; they were not supposed to travel alone; they were too delicate for controversy. Yet there she was, haranguing workers, berating politicians, attacking the "pirates," and telling women to take to the streets, all under the cover of sacred motherhood. (p. 302)

The basis of the most powerful story is personal identity. Gardner (1995) has made this assertion. He defined *personal identity stories* as "narratives that help individuals think about and feel who they are, where they come from, and where they are headed"; more than this, he attested that these stories "constitute the single most powerful weapon in the leader's literary arsenal" (p. 43). Gardner also explained that leaders have to be able to place themselves in their times with stories that convey not just a life or life experience but a "life cycle" (p. 43).

Initiation. Departure. Return. This is a life cycle. Campbell's leadership journey offers a compelling narrative about the human life cycle and struggles across culture, time, and geography. Take Mother Jones's identity story as an example. It served as a guidepost for her thoughts and actions. Early in life her entire family, husband and children included, perished in a yellow fever epidemic in Memphis, Tennessee.

Widowed and without an education, Mother Jones resorted to needle work to survive. Later she attached herself to union causes. Like Gandhi (2008), nothing much was anticipated of Mother Jones (cited in Gorn, 2001b), yet this obscure woman rose to become a beacon of the labor movement. Her identity as an activist-leader arose out of the tragedy and toil of working-class America, where her stories of survival were forged. Gritty personal identity stories became the lightning rod that emboldened her audiences.

According to Gorn (2001a), Upton Sinclair's novel *The Coal War* depicted not only the gory Colorado coal strike (1913–1914) but also Mother Jones, whom he actually knew. Rendering her a character, he sang her praises:

There broke out a storm of applause which swelled into a tumult as a little woman came forward on the platform. She was wrinkled and old, dressed in black, looking like somebody's grandmother; she was, in truth, the grandmother of hundreds of thousands of miners. (para. 1)

Stories, novelist Sinclair wrote, were Mother Jones's weapons, expressed in the strikes she led, speeches she made, and interviews she gave with presidents and leaders of industry, prisons, and camps (as cited in Gorn, 2001a). She told the miners that if they were afraid to fight, she would go at it alone; stirring the pot of protest, "her story was a veritable Odyssey of revolt" (as cited in Gorn, 2001a, para. 2).

There is a reason why we are not sharing the kind of story Mother Jones told and the stories told about her using Campbell's model, which stirs questions about how myth and action could conceivably fit. We are unable to work from complete speeches of Mother Jones because these do not exist. Her speeches were calls to action as they have come down to us.

Nonetheless, our motivation was to use Mother Jones as an exemplar because we wanted a powerful female example of the life cycle that would convey something of a personal identity story. Thus, we are not relying strictly on male examples, like Gandhi or Churchill, to make our points about heroic actions that live on in the collective imagination.

Kinds of Stories Leaders Tell

Leaders tell five basic types of stories. Crossan (1975) identified them as myth, apologue, action, satire, and parable: "Myth establishes world. Apologue defends world. Action investigates world. Satire attacks world. Parable subverts world" (p. 50). We next briefly examine each type in sequence.

Action. Think of an action narrative as the typical novel where characters are introduced around a plot or theme that presents uncertainty, ambiguity, and/or mystery. As the narrative evolves, uncertainties may be resolved, as are certain dynamics infusing characters' relationships.

Apologue. An apologue is an allegorical story with a moral. Perhaps the most famous is Plato's (427–347 B.C.) *Allegory of the Cave* (it appeared in Book VII of *The Republic*). In this text, Plato's teacher, Socrates, converses with Glaucon, a colleague. Socrates proceeds to explain using allegorical narrative.

The situation described is of a group of men who have lived in a cave all their lives, chained in such a way they see only shadows on the wall. They have not been able to look out the open mouth of the cave and see the sun or the world in any other way, only as reflected in the shadows of passersby. They come to believe that this state of affairs is "reality."

The "moral" of this story is that what is seen in the real world is not actually "real"—it is only a representation of a facsimile of the real world. The "real" world is only one of ideas, and only ideas are true.

Sontag (1977) disputed this Platonic allegory and its devaluing of images:

> The powers of photography have in effect de-Platonized our understanding of reality, making it less and less plausible to reflect upon our experience according to the distinction between images and things, between copies and originals. It suited Plato's derogatory attitude toward images to liken them to shadows—

transitory, minimally informative, immaterial, impotent co-presences of the real things which cast them. (pp. 179–180)

The point is that photographs make shadows real by freezing them and providing something that is permanent instead of fleeting. This literary photographer underscored this point:

> But the force of photographic images comes from their being material realities in their own right, richly informative deposits left in the wake of whatever emitted them, potent means for turning the tables on reality—for turning it into a shadow. (Sontag, 1977, p. 180)

What Sontag is expressing is that the separation of reality and nonreality in this allegory is actually bridged when the "shadow" is a photograph, for a photo has a reality all its own.

Myth. In their classic work, American cognitive linguists Lakoff and Johnson (1980) wrote about myth: "All cultures have myths, and people cannot function without myth any more than they can function without metaphor. And just as we often take the metaphors of our own culture as truths, so we often take the myths of our own culture as truths" (p. 186). Truth is based on someone's grasp of a situation and the fit of that person's understanding with context.

Based on Campbell's meta analysis of myths from all over the world, myths are not lies; rather, they are stories humans tell, and have told through time, to forge understandings of the forces impacting human life. The effort is to make sense of what appears to be beyond comprehension, recognize the tensions in polar opposites, and feel enlivened and connected to creative potential.

The word *myth* is derived from the Greek word *muthos,* meaning "word," "speech," or "the thing spoken" (Larue, 1975, p. 5). Larue described the significance of myth as inextricably related to attempts to explain "why life is as it is and what man's significance is" and to understand

> that to be human, to be alive, and to have purpose is to move beyond the bounds of animal existence. Myth supports existing social structure, patterns of belief and conduct and the current interpretation of the world. At the same time, myth tends to program attitudes of individuals and groups to encourage an uncritical acceptance of the established norms of the particular society. (p. 9)

Citing eminent anthropologist Claude Levi-Strauss (1967), Crossan (1975) states that "myth performs the specific task of mediating irreducible opposites" (p. 51). Examples of such binary opposites are hot and cold and life and death. In the case of the former, a warm temperature would mediate the extremes. In the case of life and death, spirits could be a mediator.

Myth stories make big concepts like life, death, and loss more comprehensive but not less mysterious. Mythic stories are important for children to learn from because they tend to think in binaries, and while myth stories are built on binaries, they are also shrouded in mystery (Scott, 2003), forcing the imagination to be at play.

Myth has been described in almost poetic terms, as a kind of "chant in which mankind harmonizes the vagaries of history—the chant hummed for generations in the minds of men and humming itself in the human mind (that innate dream to reduce continuous randomness to a final pattern" (Crossan, 1975, p. 54).

Categories of myths include:

1. *Cosmological:* Explains some sort of cosmic order and how the world came into existence
2. *Societal:* Explains how certain social groups began in the world and describes proper conduct within them
3. *Identity:* Involves how individuals come to recognize their place as human beings
4. *Eschatological:* Deals with the finality of time and "life-death-resurrection" scenarios
5. *Death of god:* Describes symbols of human alienation
6. *Future:* Involves emerging mythic patterns "that may become dominant in the future" (Larue, 1975, p. 21)

Campbell's work combines all of these categories into universal themes of myth and story—our touchstone.

We note here that there is a delicate line between mythology and religion. Religions are forms of a living mythology—that is, they involve narratives that provide meaning to human life. The fact that they are "living" means that humans try to be congruent with those narratives. Even Max Weber (1991/ 1922) in his classic book *The Sociology of Religion* observed that "religiously or magically motivated behavior is relatively rational behavior" (p. 1) because it adheres to the laws of human experience.

A parallel form of Campbell's universal leadership journey is the idea of progress, which has deep religious roots. It is the notion that through acts of faith humans become morally better—they are on a path to perfection. It is manifested in the idea that tomorrow is going to be better than today, or that if we behave according to the tenets of faith we will reach a better place, either Nirvana or Heaven.

Nisbet (1970) says of this precept that "quite obviously so sweeping a proposition as the idea of progress . . . cannot be empirically or logically verified" (p. 6). The distinction is that while both mythology and religion use narratives to explain and guide humans, the notion of a journey can be subjected to observation and logical analysis. As exemplified in Campbell's (e.g., 2008) work, the journey motif does not slide into ritualized practices or become a form of dogma, which preclude or eliminate alternative forms of explanation. And, more importantly, it is not centered in worship.

Parable. Crossan (1975) states that *parable* is the opposite of *myth.* It is not, however, *anti-myth*; rather, "it is a story deliberately calculated to show the limitations of myth" and to shatter the world as we know it (p. 60). While the purpose of myth is to establish relationships, make connections, and justify social conventions, the function of parable is to undermine those conventions and call them into question.

Among the great parablers who have come down to us in history is Jesus of Nazareth, who worked in both deed and text as a parabler. Jesus defied many social conventions of his time. A radical of the first order, he was "more terrifying than anything we have ever imagined, and even if we can never accept it, we should not explain it away as something else" (Crossan, 1994, p. 73).

Crossan is referring to Jesus's radicality in his times and context. Jesus was far more radical than we understand today. The practice of "open commensality"—in such forms as inclusivity, as in inviting unmarried women to eat at the same table as men—is signified defiance of the extant social conventions of the times. Crossan (1994) says that "open commensality is the symbol and embodiment of radical egalitarianism, of an absolute equality of people that denies the validity of any discrimination between them and negates the necessity of any hierarchy among them" (p. 71). This is why Jesus was so threatening to the conventional notions of his times.

Jesus was a social change agent who used parable incisively, conjuring images and examples so powerful that many were remembered in oral tradition with astonishing accuracy decades after his death (Funk et al., 1993). Among the most remembered of Jesus's parables, which experts agree was most likely actually told by him, is found in Luke 10:30–35. The Good Samaritan story appears today as a *metaphor* in such mainstream publications as the *Wall Street Journal* (Rosen, 2013, p. C3).

The background for the story is that in an exchange with a lawyer, Jesus was asked, "How do you read what is written in the Law?" Roughly paraphrased, Jesus answered that people must love God with their heart and soul and their neighbor. Jesus was then asked something akin to "But who is your neighbor?" Therein ensues the story of the Good Samaritan.

The travelogue goes something like this: A man, traveling from Jerusalem to Jericho, was set upon by robbers. He was beaten, stripped of his clothes, and left to die in a ditch. A priest came upon him, not even pausing to help. Someone else actually moved to the opposite side of the road to avoid him.

In contrast, a Samaritan (an enemy of the Judeans) stopped. He bandaged the man's wounds and took him to a nearby inn. The Samaritan rented a room for him to recuperate, telling the innkeeper he would be back shortly to cover any additional expenses incurred in caring for the wounded.

The neighbor is in reality one's enemy; listeners of the day would have understood this about this story. This may be lost to us today—that "neighbor," as operationalized in the parable revealed in Luke, is not your friend but your enemy. It would be akin to something like a U.S. Marine in Afghanistan being robbed and beaten on a street in Kabul and being ignored by fellow Marines (the neighbor), but attended to by a member of the Taliban (the enemy). Jesus's message was that you must love your neighbor even if that person is your enemy.

When one loves one's neighbor as oneself and that person turns out to be your enemy, then we have the quick turn going on. This undermines what we thought was the main message in the story. The listener does not expect an enemy to extend charity and compassion or provide vigil and care. It should not come as a surprise but does that our neighbor is not like you or me, yet we can sometimes receive help from where it is least expected.

A parable, simply another method of storytelling, involves a trip wire. Crossan (1975) suggests that the function of a parable is to get "into the hearer's consciousness and it is only felt in its full force there when it is too late to do much about it" (p. 86). The idea is that myth functions to connect disparate things, whereas parables undermine and dispute those connections (Crossan & Campbell, 2008). The turning back of an expected narrative line within a story, that is, the anticipated outcome or explanation, on itself puts the whole into question.

Satire. Satire comes from the Latin word *satura,* referring to a kind of poetry in Roman society that was dramatic, then didactic (Andrews, 1854). Today it is a kind of narrative that holds up a situation or person to ridicule or scorn. Radical activist Saul Alinsky (1971) indicated in *Rules for Radicals* that "humor is essential to a successful tactician, for the most potent weapons known to mankind are satire and ridicule" (p. 75).

Alinsky used both in his struggle with the Eastman Kodak company in Rochester, New York. The conflict was over the racial integration of the workforce of this film-and-camera giant. Alinsky remarked about the Fortune 500 company that "the only contribution the Eastman Kodak company has ever made to race relations is the invention of color film" (as cited in Horwitt, 1989, p. 493). This statement delivered a jolt in a way that simple criticism would never approach. The remark was sharp and biting—such is the nature of ridicule and satire.

COLLAPSING OBJECTIVITY AND SUBJECTIVITY IN IMAGE

The data (images) from our study are situated in a view that human culture and language are contextually centered, like Lakoff and Johnson (1980) pointed out:

> We have seen that truth is relative to understanding, which means that there is no absolute standpoint from which to obtain absolute objective truths about the world. This does not mean that there are no truths; it means only that truth is relative to our conceptual system, which is grounded in, and constantly tested by, our experiences and those of other members of our culture in our daily interactions with other people and with our physical and cultural environments. (p. 193)

We do not take the view, then, that our data can be understood in terms that necessitate some sort of fixed and absolute truths as in the Platonic sense. With photographs, the bifurcation between objectivity and subjectivity collapses. Photographs represent partial truths, not the whole truth. As Becker (1978) explains,

> Every photograph, because it begins with the light rays something emits hitting film, must in some obvious sense be true; and because it could always have been made differently than it was, it cannot be the whole truth and in that sense is false. (p. 10)

In this sense, the use of photographic data involves a paradox, meaning that it is simultaneously true and false, which defies intuition and logic (see Mullen, 2011, for a discussion of paradox relative to public schooling and education leadership). Rather than being objective in the traditional sense of objectivity, the data and, in this case, photographic data are perspectival and "true" only by understanding the standpoint from which it arises (English, 1988).

RELEASING THE POWER OF METAPHORS IN LEADERSHIP

Our respondents' leadership stories were prompted by images that they translated linguistically and emotionally. The bigger picture of this connection is that ideas about purpose and identity, and ultimately about learning and leadership, emerged. Lumby and English (2010), on the topic of metaphors of educational leadership, described language and leadership as "inseparable":

> Leaders traffic in language. It is language that defines problems and solutions. It is language that stirs the imagination, defines critical issues, creates collective consciousness in followers, and frames agendas for individual and collec-

tive action, whether proactive or reactive. Language is the ultimate form of the construction of symbolic power, the means to stir humanity to pursue conquest, manage change, right perceived wrongs, find compassion for the fallen, or confront impossible odds. (p. 1)

Metaphors of management, administration, and leadership have been employed to conceptualize school leadership. The literature in leadership has advanced the notion that metaphors are intrinsic in the work of leaders. Metaphors inspire and motivate beyond "checklists and management plans"—they require "an interactive and dynamic presence, an ability to turn a key phrase in order to prod or inspire people to think beyond themselves" (Lumby & English, 2010, p. 5), just as we attempted to do with this study.

Metaphors play expansive and restrictive roles in leadership theory and practice. Notably, metaphors can "be used as a tool for human development, locating leadership within a mythological universe, and not just a political and social one" (Lumby & English, 2010, p. 6).

Just as metaphors can be used to inspire or motivate, they can also be used to obstruct or misdirect; hence the purpose of metaphors can vary considerably. And sometimes, we recognize, the purpose of metaphors is simply unknown or multifaceted.

Prevalent metaphors from the educational leadership research include:

- organization as educational community (e.g., Beck, 1999; Sergiovanni & Corbolly, 1984); and
- administration as putting out fires, that is, moving from one (minor) urgency to the next in an effort to stabilize a situation or workplace (e.g., Weick, 1996).

Another popular image, although perhaps not self-evident, is purpose, maintenance, and survival (see Bredeson, 1985, on these images from the perspectives of school principals and see Ylimaki, 2006, on the image of vision).

With buy-in from a faculty perspective is the metaphor of educational leadership as being at a crossroads (with regard to external and political pressures to prepare educational leaders differently) (English, Papa, Mullen, & Creighton, 2012; Hackman & McCarthy, 2011), or "crossing" in Campbell's mythic lexicon of the phases of the life journey. An example of being at the crossroads involves the visibility/invisibility paradox for leaders of color in the struggle for fairness and "equitable recognition" (Bloom & Erlandson, 2003; Mullen & Robertson, 2014).

The tension between invisibility and visibility underscores the roles of leadership for women of color who are marginalized in society. This status is mirrored in their leadership of predominantly White school organizations. Visibility requires that they shift their identities either to accommodate dominant behavioral norms outside their home codes or to resist these norms. Activism favors counter-stories that push against the status quo and change work cultures.

Mullen and Robertson (2014) offer identity stories from the perspectives of female principals of color for whom identity development as a leader involves high levels of risk-taking in a world where complexity, ambiguity, and uncertainty are professional norms. Nuances surround shifting identities from one context to the next, and interpretations rely on perceived factors in the external environment, such as the mental mindset and biases of stakeholders.

Tooms, Lugg, and Bogotch (2010), describing fit, identified it as "the tension between the socially constructed roles of leadership and a leader's decision to observe, subvert, or transcend these roles determines how we assess a leader's fit" (p. 106). The phenomena of fit (Tooms et al., 2010) and of shifting (Mullen & Robertson, 2014) require that the leader deal with aporia—the space between two worlds (e.g., external and internal). This lived tension must be constantly negotiated in the journey of leaders.

We would be remiss not to spend time with the metaphor of machine, likely the most commonly used metaphor of all in the education leadership field. More and more machine-like, leaders have been likened to efficiency figures such as an "inspector and quality controller" whose thoughts and behaviors are mechanistic, communicating an "adherence to procedures that are standardized and detached from human judgment" (Lumby & English, 2010, p. 6).

The machine, connoting efficiency, looms as a negative mental mindset in the award-winning article by Tooms et al. (2010). A pocket watch (both described and sketched) with "only one hand, an hour hand" provokes questions about how leaders understand their daily work lives and whether the behaviors they expect and that are expected of them are stagnant, even when socially constructed (p. 106).

This is where the idea of fit comes in. The point of reference of the watch piece with the single hand is presented as terribly limiting. In the efficiency world of one hand, one way of knowing, there is a deadening point of reference from which leaders understand themselves and their world, which serves as a resounding warning:

> Over time, we will get used to this watch and it will become normal to tell time with just this one hand. Our single-hand watch remains our everyday reference for telling time. We stop thinking in terms of minutes or seconds and just accept the hours as our common sense of reality. When the single hand points up, it is midday or midnight. There is no half past, quarter past, 5 minutes till. We become confident in our ability to tell time, and why not? The hour hand becomes good enough. (p. 106)

Thus, the metaphor of efficiency underscores the need for new ways of thinking that counter restrictive ways of knowing, thinking, and acting in one's leadership and work with others. As Tooms et al. (2010) asked, "Might our measures of fit in terms of leadership be one dimensional and render invisible the very dynamics we most need to improve schools?" (p. 106)

The "pedagogical machine" Lumby and English (2010, p. 6) identify is a spinoff metaphor. It connotes teaching to the test. Despite the fact that *pedagogy* means "teaching," the pedagogical machine does not uphold humanistic values and learning but instead turns children's ability to perform into a prescriptive set of actions governed by standardized assessment and a compulsive nationwide neurosis surrounding competitive performance by students, schools, and states.

Efficiency metaphors of leadership are also captured by Lumby and English's (2010) metaphor of leader as accountant. The accountant compulsively measures school improvement and student growth through reductive means, such as annual yearly performance markers and testing scores, while missing a myriad of possibilities for teaching and learning.

The leader as warrior in the Lumby and English (2010) metaphoric lexicon refers to the Western approach to competitive behavior, which is different from Eastern understandings of spirituality linked with warrior. Sports metaphors reduce *leader* to *coach* and import "unrealistic notions of heroic leadership and a history of sexism" (p. 7). The metaphor of "education leadership as theater" refers to the role of the leader relative to different audiences, scripts, and stages (p. 7).

Metaphors of religion in educational leadership underscore the moral, ethical, and spiritual role of leaders but are also used within some education management standards to perpetuate notions that reek of "metaphysical beliefs and assumptions. These are often unsupported by any kind of evidence, sometimes they exist in flat contradiction to such evidence as is available" (Pattison, 1997, p. 26).

Look out for the leader who is a lunatic! Such leaders have been described as "instrumentally impulsive individuals with poor behavioral controls who callously and remorselessly bleed others for purely selfish reasons via manipulation, intimidation, and violence" (Hamilton, 2008, p. 232).

The inclusion of this idea by Lumby and English (2010) provokes readers to stand back and take note. It warns us about pathological forces that squash the human agency of leaders and that they themselves squash without even knowing it. Leadership gone bad seriously impacts culture by infusing "a range of disordered behaviors, sociopathic attitudes to faculty and to children, the fetishistic engagement with statistics, and other seemingly pathological behaviors" (p. 7).

The power of metaphor in leadership honors the perpetual gap between theory and practice without reducing or collapsing the tensions they share.

For decades, educational leadership programs have been seriously criticized for failing to teach aspiring administrators practical ideas for "solving real problems in the field" (Murphy & Forsyth, 1999, p. 15).

Lortie (1998) attests that practice in the form of field-based conceptual and social skills—such as interpreting school data—is critical to the work of school leaders. Educational theory has no real role with this emphasis on practice, which perpetuates the schism between practice and theory. The use of metaphor brings theory and practice into a relationship (Mullen, Greenlee, & Bruner, 2005), which is not the same thing as a simple alignment.

Models, such as the universal journey myth, and organizing principles that include conceptual schemes and evocative metaphors should not have to be separated from practice. To bring theory and practice into new relationships would open up renewed possibilities for theoretical representations and practical applications.

Life as a journey is the main metaphor we are using in this book because it is the one that is rife with possibility in the mental mappings of leaders and relative to our model of cognitive aesthetics. Lakoff and Johnson (1980) posit that metaphorical mappings, such as life as a journey, refer to the intricate structures of our language systems. Metaphor can be used to capture a flexible, creative, and analytic form of integration in educational theory and practice, as well as in thought and action.

When metaphors do not express a single proposition, alternative meanings become possible and may be expressed and realized. Thus the power of metaphors in leadership offers new possibilities for conceptualizing school leadership. Exploring the theory-practice relationship enables people to probe the tension between these aspects and their inseparableness, which honors complexity in meaning-making, distinguishing this relationship from simple integration (Mullen et al., 2005).

An interpretation along these lines honors tensions and complexity in meaning-making, distinguishing the theory-practice relationship from being thought of as simple integration. As simple integration, the relationship remains atomized, an under-theorized conception of human thought and action. As a concept of embeddedness, the theory-practice relationship in leadership expands possibilities for imagining the role of cognitive aesthetics through narrative and metaphor.

Leadership dialogue and work employ narrative and metaphor. Leaders traffic in signs and symbols and must constantly make meaning and interpret ambiguity. The technical metaphors of teaching and learning that prevail in our discipline obstruct reflection and inquiry and dissuade alternatives and possibilities.

The metaphor of leadership as a compass has been used to orient discourse about social (in)justices as educational leadership constructs and actions (Mullen, Young, & Harris, 2014). The compass construct has the directional needles of consciousness-raising among leaders in educational spaces and social justice advocacy in schools, communities, and legislatures.

The idea is for difficult conversations, integrated within social justice frameworks, to become part of leadership programs, professional development agendas, and life within schools and communities. More discourse is needed on the subject of difficult cultural conversation within a changing global economy for the benefit of educational stakeholders and communities. We elaborate on these points as related to trust-building for leaders in chapter 4.

For this study, we have tried out an artful demonstration of the process of inquiry that could help leaders conceptualize issues of context and culture and think about the subjectivity at work within their administrative roles and potential for artistry. Artistry can be reflected in many ways, including leaders' narratives, decisions, and actions. We are writing about aspects of visual data and the process of interpretation from an arts-based perspective for educational leadership. This perspective is linked to the value of storytelling for leaders and the stories of their followers.

To quote an anonymous reviewer of our preliminary writing, these were all lessons drawn:

> Leaders like stories; leaders tell stories. Leaders use stories to make a point—to drive an agenda, to get people to listen, and to inspire. A focus on the self and mythology is a natural for current and future school leaders who not only lead with their stories; they learn from the stories of each other. (May 2013)

About another dynamic, we were aware that the interpretation of visual data in our study is connected to class and culture. Bourdieu (1984) found that people of higher social classes are more apt to construct abstract meanings from photographs, rather than relying on literal or conventional interpretation. This analysis was entirely appropriate for this inquiry in that the individual practicing administrators, though diverse by gender and race, were of similar social class.

We assumed the leaders would be able to interpret the photographs using the symbols (e.g., casket) and universal themes (e.g., life, death, loss, and the struggle to overcome adversity). Not only did we find this assumption warranted, but also their sensemaking was such that they used some of the images for more than one benchmark of the leadership journey. Regarding the potential we saw for these leaders to make sense of myths using visual images, according to photographer Cartier-Bresson (1998), photography naturally elicits interpretation—this medium aids recognition of human rhythms and cycles.

Artists generally appreciate the power of subjectivity in their work, unlike many professionals who are simply not on the path toward understanding their interiority. In Campbell's (2008) worldview, there are those who have refused to accept or respond to a calling:

> Often in actual life, and not infrequently in the myths and popular tales, we encounter the dull case of the call unanswered; for it is always possible to turn the ear to other interests. Refusal of the summons converts the adventure into its negative. Walled in boredom, hard work or "culture," the subject loses the power of significant affirmative action and becomes a victim to be saved. (p. 49)

Ignoring the calling and becoming a victim makes people suffer. Researchers perpetuate the suffering of the self in the effort to "bracket" their subjectivity (Halling, Leifer, & Rowe, 2006). From this perspective, one's identity is subsumed—or is thought to be—by the presumption that the researcher can bracket or set aside his or her experiences, as well as beliefs, assumptions, values, and biases. A false claim is that there is no claim to make. Another false claim is that data can be read for data's sake, as though issues of identity can be stripped from data interpretation.

In contrast, artists and activists take it upon themselves to challenge the objectivist ideology that has claimed their identity and, in effect, has blocked awareness of their beliefs, assumptions, values, and biases (Ehrich & English, 2013). Critical theorists Halling et al. (2006) state that such understanding is necessary for acknowledging how deeply these affect knowledge construction and power relations. Such understanding is also necessary if you are to experience what Campbell describes as affirmative action to any degree of significance.

How might educational leaders benefit, then, from understanding their leadership in mythic and situated, subjective and aesthetic terms? In contrast with superficial and compartmentalized thinking that can lead to inhumane action, we join that growing league of activist scholars committed to seeking tools that advance understanding of leadership not only as situated-universal knowing but also as an art or performance. Engaging in "an identity performance" where leaders act the self, they position themselves to "enact a self-aware leadership" (Lumby & English, 2009, p. 1).

However, the inner value of educational leaders is being neglected and their subjectivity devalued; instead they are immersed in achieving purposes of outer value through policy benchmarks for which they are thoroughly conditioned. The principal measure of success in American public schools continues to be standardized test scores. This measure has been critiqued as shallow and undemocratic, an obfuscation of the realities of leadership in schools and unthinking reinforcement of the factory model of schooling (Shields & Mohan, 2008).

More than ever, leaders who refuse to have the subjectivities of their community demeaned are being forced to display civic courage in confronting the coercive powers that influence their contexts and people's lives. Because oppressive circumstances can deplete creative resources and will-power, and because we all have personal limitations, leaders must continual-ly reinvent themselves and their world (English, 2008b; Lumby & English, 2009; Mullen, 2008).

Mohandas Gandhi had to confront his personal fears and physical limita-tions. Yet his global vision for social justice functioned contagiously as memes (ideas) through other people who cared about moral goodness. While Gandhi believed that leaders are not to be blamed for their social condition-ing, they nonetheless must determine to change systemic injustices by re-flecting on and interrogating their values, biases, and actions (see English 2008a; 2008b).

Applied to the educational leadership field, Gandhi's wisdom exposes cultural deficits. First, internal issues are inadequately explored in our profes-sion, despite the call for meaningful dialogue about the preparation of educa-tional leaders (see Mullen, English, Brindley, Ehrich, & Samier, 2013).

Second, practically speaking, the human agency of educational leadership programs needs to be reclaimed, as the programs are being pushed away from rigor and vibrancy toward externally controlled, superficial expressions of leadership: "The new rhetoric of consumerism and the market metaphors aimed at 'bottom-line' thinking are propelling the profession" toward the "profit motive" and launching "a full-scale assault on the service ethic of the profession" (English, 2006, p. xxxvi). How can leadership faculty model through our research and teaching an honoring of the "inner value" of leader-ship without ignoring the external value?

Some leadership preparation scholars are attempting to create subjective-ly aware "democratically accountable leaders" (Mullen, 2008, p. 137) who understand that their knowing is constituted in relation to power, hierarchy, and authority. From this viewpoint, the leader of schools will have to con-stantly negotiate the tension between democracy and accountability in their decision-making and choices. Leadership faculty face the same struggle in their courses.

Some educational leadership preparation programs struggle with translat-ing transformative identity models (such as democratically accountable lead-ership) into curriculum that aids personal discovery for aspiring leaders (Mullen, Harris, Pryor, & Browne-Ferrigno, 2008). The reality is that their mental models involving high-stakes accountability and managerial ap-proaches for achieving a results-driven culture are simultaneously being shaped by social and political systems (Mullen et al., 2014).

Progressive leaders may realize that gender, along with race and social class, is a social construct that can promote or marginalize individuals and groups, thus granting or barring privilege. And they know that stereotypes about males and females promote a double standard in work settings *and* that these beliefs are encoded from within, manifesting in not just how gender is viewed but also how it is enacted (Blount, 2005).

But are such leaders aware of their own human sensemaking in the process of decision formulation and execution? Leaders can benefit from the arts in this respect too. The arts have the great potential to aid in the discovery process that is conducive to better understanding interiority (Ribbins, 2006).

It is from the arts that the metaphors of the larger motifs of life are captured and discussed. These are the themes that connect leaders and followers emotionally and that are the cornerstone of the establishment of trust. It is the idea that we all stand on the same ground and share a common human condition.

A view of the human condition was captured for the respondents by the image of African Americans walking along a river as the photo that embodied the idea of life being a journey—literally, a path taken. With some diversity and variation as the backdrop to a somewhat similar thought process, the school leaders also revealed insight into the human condition and the other phases of the journey motif. This implies resonance and perhaps even underlying symmetry.

Campbell's (2008) idea of life being a universally experienced journey filled with struggle, hardship, and even happiness was implied by the respondents' resonating stories of life. Their selection of photos and associations with them evoked not only reverberation across the interviews but also similar understandings, overlapping experiences, and deep empathy. Similarly, the other photographs captured states of despair as well as of hope in very hard times, and the recognition of significant trials that bond human beings across time and space.

The data from this study validated the following major phases in Campbell's universal leadership journey:

- challenges involving the universal human condition;
- personal trials that all humans face;
- human transformation as part of the process of the leadership journey; and
- crossing important thresholds in the leadership journey.

School leaders identified as important markers in Campbell's universal leadership journey how the image related to their own leadership career, whether the image reminded them of important passages or problems, and if so, what those were. We specifically discovered that the leaders were able to relate to the universal life journey model and across the six defining phases (i.e., human condition, trials in life, human triumph, human transformation, human crossing, and leadership). This resonance with the phases implied universality of experience. Further, we identified common characteristics of their journeys.

Our interviews with the school principals and district leaders surfaced their struggle of constantly being in a hurried state in the work environment at the expense of doing inner, transformational work. Leaders who are active learners reflect on the meaning of their work relative to broader questions about the purpose of life, and they widen the circle for advocacy and agency beyond themselves (Gardner, 1995).

It became clear to us that school leaders live in multiple worlds that are both highly rational and highly emotional, as well as personal. The tension between these two worlds is constant. The rational, economic, and logical world resonates to facts and figures—highly quantitative information now called "big data" in the popular press. Yet, despite all of the number-crunching, it is easy to get lost in the other world, that which is intensely cultural, contextual, and personal. And indeed that subjective world is never really "lost" in the traditional sense. Accordingly, as Lumby and Coleman (2007) argue,

> Much normative leadership and management literature assumes a rational ap-
> proach to assessing situations and in response taking logical actions for the
> benefit of the organization and/or its clients. However, numerous writers have
> stressed that the platform of apparent conscious rationality floats on a sea of
> often unconscious irrationality. (p. 31)

The use of highly emotive visual data in our study broke open and exposed deep underlying resonances that are part of humanity's common heritage, serving as a poignant place to stop and contemplate its presence in our lives. How we deal with our common humanity in preparation programs for educational leaders is the matter we next discuss.

Key Concepts

Aporia. As described by Jacques Derrida (1930–2004), aporia is "a way of thinking, the possibility of impossibility" rejecting any binary logic (as cited in Peeters, 2013, p. 449) and dealing with the phenomenon of contradiction. An aporia is the space between borders, categories, domains, or knowledge disciplines in which such distinctions can be dissolved or deconstructed.

Code. The code implies patterns ordinary people use in constructing collections of snapshots (photographic data) for display in scrapbooks or other home memorabilia (see Chalfen, 2001). The importance of code is that a snapshot's "meaning" is defined by the narrative or story in which it is embedded. Meaning is provided by the narrative.

Fit. The extent to which the narratives of a potential leader match those in an audience of listeners is determined by how well the story or elements of the story are already known by the audience (Gardner, 1995). Simple stories are ones that most often prevail.

Metaphor. A metaphor is a linguistic device in which two things are compared that "are similar and dissimilar. The reader or listener is thrown into a state of momentary uncertainty, where the degree and significance of the similarity and dissimilarity must be considered" (Lumby & English, 2010, p. 3). Lakoff and Johnson (1980) indicate that "the essence of metaphor is understanding and experiencing one kind of thing in terms of another" (p. 5).

Objectivity. The myth of objectivity indicates that the world is made up of objects that "have properties independent of any people or other beings who experience them" (Lakoff & Johnson, 1980, p. 186); the myth posits that "there is an objective reality, and we can say things that are objectively, absolutely and unconditionally true and false about it" (p. 187).

Personal identity stories. The purpose of narratives is to get in touch with who a person is in the present, who s/he was in the past, and who s/he will be in the future. The life span and life cycle of a person and the life cycles of humanity are interconnected through personal identity stories (Gardner, 1995).

Realism. With photography, an image is considered "real" if it corresponds to the "actual features of the world" as understood by the viewer (Little, 1999, p. 706). Purists of this perspective do not approve of any altering of an image once it is photographed.

Subjectivity. The myth of subjectivity indicates that "the most important things in our lives are our feelings, aesthetic sensibilities, moral practices and spiritual awareness" and "in matters of personal understanding the ordinary agreed-upon meanings that words have will not do" (Lakoff & Johnson, 1980, p. 188).

Total configuration. This involves human beings perceiving a situation as a totality within a kind of "silent language" of emotion and gestures, cultural and social contexts (Drucker, 1974).

Types of stories. Crossan (1975) identified five types of stories told by leaders: action, apologue, myth, parable, and satire.

We next turn to chapter 4, where we deal specifically with the data we collected and analyzed relative to leadership practice.

Chapter Four

Describing the Triad of Trust for Leadership Practice

Emotion is essential to the life journey of leaders. Where there is *trust*, leaders are bonded to followers. Followers are bonded to leaders. A trusting culture can make the kinds of profound differences we discuss in this chapter.

We describe dynamics relevant to the building of trusting cultures herein but begin with the premise that the most fundamental shift in leadership practice from our study is the dissolution of the binary between rationality and emotionality. Herein we describe the relevance of emotionality for leadership practice by examining what we have learned about educational leaders' vision of key elements of leadership today.

Of course leaders are emotional because they are human. But one won't find that aspect of leadership in any national (or state) standards for educational leaders, nor in the emerging metrics for how leaders are evaluated or paid (for a critique of state and national stands in educational leadership, see English, 2008a).

From the research we conducted and reported in this book, we believe that our primary finding is the restoration of what influential management guru Douglas McGregor (1960/2006) described over fifty years ago in *The Human Side of Enterprise*, which emphasized the whole human being. He determined that what was essential for sound business practice involved not only human potential and growth, but also the human role in what was at that time an industrial society. His premise was that managers (i.e., leaders) must examine assumptions about the most effective ways to manage and motivate people, and foster humane change in the workplace.

In updating McGregor's perspective for the contemporary educational leader, we contend that the full human being—brain and heart—matters, and not just the rational but also the emotional aspects (see Bolton & English, 2009). Validating emotions is not simply an individual psychological matter, but rather a recognition in the sociology of organizations that "emotions are social constructs situated within culture and organizational contexts" (Blackmore, 2009, p. 110). As Lupton (1998) expresses,

> Emotions, therefore, are learned, contextual, and intersubjective; they are historically, socially, and politically contingent, produced by, and productive of, social and political effects at a macro as well as micro and meso levels.

The importance of emotionality in decision-making and as a social (group) phenomenon is significant in our research. In fact, Blackmore (2009) went so far as to state that education is a field of emotionality wherein emotion circulates in such a way that potentially links "individual advancement and collective improvement for marginalized social groups, promising progressive social change" (p. 116). Harding and Pribram (2004) explain,

> The circulation of emotion produces in and between people connection, ruptures, dependences, responsibilities, accountabilities, and so on. . . . [When] people care—they are invested. If people care, certain effects are produced; they feel and act in certain ways. (p. 879)

This observation was underscored in interviews with the decision-making of middle managers, such as academic department chairs. English and Bolton (2008) heard testimonies that follow about the inevitability of emotions in doing—and living out—administrative work.

> We're always emotional. We act in emotion. I try to act out of the emotion. I'm steeped in emotion. Every decision is always sitting on top of the emotion, or even enfolded in emotion. The wrong decisions of life are made in a state of emotion. My emotions today may not be my emotions tomorrow. (p. 112)

> I go with my gut a lot of the time. Afterwards I reflect on it. (p. 112)

> It's an emotional reaction. A tension you feel between what you want to do and what somebody else wants you to do. It's the tension. I find it hard to deal with. (p. 112)

As these comments convey, leadership *is* emotional work. Some leaders are comfortable with their emotions, whereas others are not, and still others recognize the ongoing push and pull of the felt dimension in the administrative arena. While they may think or act like other supervisors or peers, they may have different opinions and act independently. Examples include mandates in the areas of personnel supervision and structural operations.

The mid-level administrators from the 2008 English and Bolton study acknowledged that their emotions affected decision-making, but felt guilty about this. Many thought that allowing their emotions to enter into their roles was a negative reflection on their capacity to make decisions objectively and fairly: "I'm constantly weighing. I'm keeping my passions in check" (p. 112). Notice the distinct discomfort (i.e., emotion) in this short utterance. What role does emotion play in your decision-making?

The research we did for this book affirms the role of emotion in the lives of school administrators. In our interview sessions, emotion was channeled in responses as leaders spoke about what the images meant to them. Emotions, evoked when interpreting the images, sometimes bubbled over into speech-lessness, surprise, contemplative pauses, and even tears. Expressed were a range of emotions suggestive of sadness, caring, *compassion*, and joyfulness.

There were also breakthrough moments that registered when respondents expressed personal connections with a photo. This happened even when they were not certain who was being depicted in the photograph or the exact time period, place, event, or circumstances.

Regardless of their ability to identify the particulars of a photograph, they connected emotionally. For example, they expressed empathy in their ability to identify with or at least imagine the struggles of destitution for families enduring abject poverty, especially children living on the brink of death.

The photos the school leaders elaborated on affirmed some aspect of their work lives and, more broadly, the life journey of leaders and the cycles described by Joseph Campbell (e.g., 1972/1993). We think of leadership as passive resistance or nonviolence, as with world-renowned leaders Mahatma Gandhi and Martin Luther King Jr., whose leadership exemplifies large-scale social and political change through stoic humbleness. On the other hand, we also think of fiery leaders like Joan of Arc and Mother Jones, who led males to action despite entrenched, negative stereotypes of females.

Although the topic of sex stereotyping was not raised by our respondents, we could not help but think that providing them with examples of passive male leadership and assertive female leadership may have evoked contem-plation on perceived role-reversals. In the photos, they may have seen pos-sibilities and opportunities for themselves and the current and future leader-ship of schools.

We also recall powerful photos that forced acknowledgment of the inevi-tability of human death. Rituals, such as funerals, captured aspects of heroic action and suggested mythic presence. These images may have reminded at least a few of our respondents of how in the physical passing of a leader a life's journey has been fulfilled but the journey continues for others.

Just as our respondents recognized, the ending of a life can be tragic with devastating emotional effects—for example, an assassination or the death of a child. Perhaps sparked for them is the realization that the leadership journey continues like a pulsating river to inspire the living, some of whom take up the call and enter the currents. Against the tide, carrying on with a cause.

COMPLETION AND REALIZATION OF LIFE CYCLES

Such nonverbal reactions underscore the impossibility of fencing off human emotion from decision-making in educational administration. Trying to ignore emotions in leading schools is a fool's errand. Nothing is more rational than acknowledging that all decisions are not totally rational, and that work in schools is emotional. Decision-making is motivated by signs, symbols, and images that impact us and resonate with our lives, experiences, and identity as human beings.

Emotion lies at the heart of educational leadership—not on some periphery. It is *not* a distant cousin of thought and action. Emotion is who you are. Look within.

THE TRIAD OF TRUST AND LEADERSHIP FOR SOCIAL JUSTICE

Crawford (2009) urged educational leaders to "build a climate of genuine emotion where acceptance and trust are the building blocks of team work, and others not only want to follow them as leaders, but feel able to become leaders themselves" (pp. 192–193). Brown and Moffett (1999) envisioned a heroic system where "leaders empower school-based staff members by encouraging independence and experimentation" (p. 118).

Education is a distinctive field because, according to Todd (1997), education "assembles the affective in ways that function within power relations. Affect is central to education because it fuels the social imaginary about what education offers in terms of identity and culture" (p. 5). In other words, educational leaders are propelled by a desire to improve not only our society but also the world.

This emotion is the source of the passion for social justice advocacy. This advocacy not only critiques power relations and privilege in education and within school cultures but also energizes the social imaginary (Bogotch & Shields, 2014; Nieuwenhuizen & Brooks, 2013) through such means as exploring personal reactions to social justice agendas (e.g., becoming racially conscious, sensitive leaders of communities) directly with school leaders.

In a pedagogical study conducted by Mullen, Young, and Harris (2014), a diverse group of school leaders participated in consciousness-raising dialogue; it was found that dynamics around cultural dialogue produce emotional, personal, and political effects. The participants felt such emotions as insecurity and self-consciousness, and they silenced others or were self-silencing. The cultural discourse was seen as essential for eliciting discomfort.

The idea is that feelings of unease are a part of meaningful conversations that in turn have a greater potential for motivating leaders to pursue advocacy work in school communities.

We turn now to the triad of the trust concept, a unique feature of this book (see figure 4.1). Key to our research is the finding that emotion is the cornerstone of a leader's noncognitive life worlds. The feelings of school administrators are not peripheral to their core principles, decision-making, activism, and actions. In figure 4.1 we exhibit compassion, integrity, and wisdom within a framework in which trust serves as the nexus and synergistic glue.

In figure 4.1 note the inner portion of the triangular shape and consider its connection to reciprocity. Trust is a two-way phenomenon; followers put their trust in the leader and, correspondingly, the leader trusts that those who follow do so for the right reasons.

Figure 4.1. The Triad of Trust: Compassion, Integrity, Wisdom

Trust within organizations has two dimensions. Lateral trust is collegial or centered in a team or group of people in an organization. Vertical trust relates to those in a subordinate-superior relationship and is centered in hierarchical relationships. Chhuon, Gilkey, Gonzalez, Daly, and Chrispeels (2008) defined lateral or work-team trust as relational trust and vertical trust as managerial or leadership trust. Both dimensions are included in the triad of trust model.

Reciprocity also refers to the elements on the outside of the triangular shape: integrity, compassion, and wisdom. Would a leader whose actions are not honest gain the trust of followers? Similarly, a leader who lacks compassion probably would not earn the trust of followers. Finally, one could say the same thing regarding wisdom—who could trust the words or actions of somebody who doesn't exhibit integrity or compassion?

The interrelationship between the leader and those who follow is one born of mutual trust. We tend to look simplistically at the connection between leader and follower as a cause-effect phenomenon. The leader creates a following, but in fact the followers are as much a part of the genesis of the leader as other circumstances like epiphany/vision and fate/destiny.

Figure 4.1 does not suggest a formula for developing new leaders. Instead, it offers an open-ended framework for exploring issues and dynamics of leadership within social contexts and from a socially just perspective.

Moving this abstract concept onto a more pragmatic level, consider leadership that is socially just. What does it mean, for example, for leaders to confront issues of poverty and other inequities? In this chapter we propose that we should be looking at our leaders with a different kind of lens, one consistent with figure 4.1. How compassionate are aspiring and practicing leaders? Is integrity a core value? How wise are they?

Taken from this angle, perhaps there are ways of viewing poverty programs as something other than a social obligation or an entitlement borne of guilt; instead view them as transparent actions that spring from a commitment to compassion and integrity. When compassion has integrity and is authentic, it approaches wisdom.

Motive is the key. Integrity addresses the element of motive in one's action; it is possible to fake compassion, to appear sincere. Social climbers and careerists are only concerned about their personal game plan. Aspiring leaders of schools will naturally be concerned about their career trajectories but this should not dampen their morality or weaken their resolve to develop a social justice core. Moral compasses need to be directed toward the human side of a leader's enterprise.

Compassionate leaders do not use followers for personal gain or motive. As change agents, they try to create conditions for one individual, team, or school to have the desired influence. Highly impactful change agents work at a different scale, trying to make the world fairer and more equitable.

We made the emotions of our respondents the cornerstone of building trust, the essential ingredient to the practice of socially just leadership in schools. Trust is an active construction of interdependence between or among human beings or, in our case, an educational leader and her faculty, parents, and students. Such relationships are essential for making the impossible possible in leadership, which involves the social construction of meaning between leaders and followers.

Without trust, nothing is possible except the most superficial of managerial conformance and performance. This is usually accompanied by heavy-handed authoritarianism. With trust almost everything is possible, and leaders learn from their own mistakes and misadventures.

Making mistakes and having misadventures happens. To err is human. Followers, too, will make mistakes or be perceived as erring. Compassion in leadership recognizes this. Followers, such as teachers, have a greater chance of succeeding when their mistakes are constructively addressed, such as missing a critical deadline that somehow disadvantages staff or students. Realities of failures ranging from misfortunes to missteps are at the heart of organizational learning and improved organizational performance, and these dynamics are an inescapable part of heroic action.

Components of the Trust Framework

The triad of trust requires at least three components. First is compassion. This human emotion involves sympathy and understanding, just as caring does, but it also embodies the compunction to act on those feelings.

As described by English (2008a), compassion goes beyond caring: Not only does compassion mean the "sympathetic consciousness of others' distress together with a desire to alleviate it" (Merriam-Webster, 2003) but also the agency expressed by actions taken to improve the lives and circumstances of other human beings, such as poverty and inequity, and on a larger scale than one's small world.

Compassionate leaders are human agents of change. They are benevolent, reliable, competent, honest, and open; they do not exploit others and, moreover, they accept responsibility. Importantly, they are authentic, truth-telling individuals (Bennis, 1997; Tschannen-Moran, 2001; 2004; 2009) who strive to model this way of life for others.

The second component of trust is integrity. Compassion requires integrity, also known as transparency, which is the capacity for being open to truth(s) and for being truthful. Perhaps the closest we might come to this meaning of integrity or transparency is Gandhi's notion (as cited in Iyer, 1973/2000) of *ahimsa*. Translated, *ahimsa* is "the largest love, the greatest charity" that encompasses truth and fearlessness (p. 180; see also English, 2008a).

We see wisdom as the third component of trust. Historian Lawrence (2011), known as the "Lawrence of Arabia," describes in his famous book *Seven Pillars of Wisdom* (first appearing in 1922) the presence of compassion and integrity in wisdom, whether in battle or in life. Tschannen-Moran (2004), in her work on school-based leadership, states that wisdom plays a crucial role in supporting as well as challenging the people in one's domain to change.

Lawrence (2001) and Tschannen-Moran (2004), although from different worlds and oddly juxtaposed in time, both view wisdom as a strong leadership quality. Wisdom enables leaders to navigate complex decisions and life choices, no matter how difficult. Wise leaders, such as the biblical character of Solomon, displayed wisdom through an interest in education and by raising questions about moral choices and ethical conduct (Lawrence, 2011).

In *The Wit and Wisdom of Gandhi* (Jack, 1951/1979), Gandhi's concepts of wisdom took the form of a diet rich in social and personal ethics. Contributing writer John Haynes Holmes, Harvard University divinity scholar and recipient of the Gandhi Peace Award, endorses this viewpoint. Jack's book stimulates readers to think in theoretical and practical terms about what we term the "Gandhi dialectic," which, building on Holmes's and Jack's reflections, involves a lifelong preparation of the self and others for opposing oppression while envisioning and working toward freedom.

Examples from Jack's (1951/1979) book as applied to leadership contexts encompass the heroic actions of leaders that

- foster conditions for communal unity and shared profound commitments;
- confront as well as change oppressive forces of poverty, racism, and bigotry;
- represent underrepresented populations in the body politic (e.g., school governance);
- adopt nonviolent stances no matter the level of threat and potential violence; and
- practice humane leadership in the effort to advance trust and affection.

Based on this way of thinking, the humane treatment of people by leaders and followers multiplies many times over and strengthens the whole. With regard to social transformation in Gandhi's life-world and legacy, the message of nonviolence in particular shines through: "Gandhi's greatest social invention was *satyagraha*," described as a group's nonviolent actions that perpetuate "a soul force" (Jack, 1951/1979, p. 7).

While wisdom is elusive, making it especially hard to discern as a component of trust, it can be felt, probably even seen, especially in our rearview mirror. Wisdom is crucial to the daily activity and transformative work of leaders and followers. Wisdom comes in many stripes, not only moral wisdom but also political wisdom and private wisdom. Private wisdom allows leaders to describe difficult circumstances to their stakeholders without making them fearful of change.

Wise leaders help people to maintain perspective when feeling challenged or overwhelmed, to learn from their mistakes and misadventures, as well as to become more intelligent by creating meaning out of circumstances. Wise leaders also create spaces for new possibilities to emerge. This helps people to imagine a better world while seeking more effective ways of doing business.

Wisdom helps all leaders to lead with compassion and integrity, to make meaning out of bleakness and see hope in despair, to use core ethics and values in all crucial negotiations and decision-making, and to take action even while stepping into that always-uncertain future.

The wisdom of Gandhi is not for saints—it is for everyone, all people. Caring leaders who do not cultivate vision, hope, and faith will falter and be ineffectual. Leaders who use the rhetoric of wisdom (such as that of social justice) but who fail to take constructive action in the face of intense discomfort fall short of helping people to realize or, better yet, exercise their own wisdom.

At the core of *leadership for social justice* is trust. We think that change requires focus from compassionate leaders and dynamics of trust in community or context. Trust is an essential concept of leadership for community-building and civic service.

When we think of trust, we must also consider human emotion in leadership, expressed in our research in the faces staring back from iconic photographs etched with hardship from poverty, devastation from loss, courage in the political arena, rage at society, and love of humankind. Social justice involves trust—it is inextricably connected to the human, organizational, and cultural catalysts of compassion, integrity, and wisdom.

Research on trust and social justice has been sporadically explored in the education field. Perhaps at the helm is educational leadership professor Megan Tschannen-Moran. Tschannen-Moran (2004), as well as Bennis (1997) and Putnam and Feldstein (2003), explained that there is a trend away from trust in communities and schools.

Harvard University public policy professor Robert Putnam (e.g., Putnam & Feldstein, 2003) argues, "Beginning, roughly speaking, in the late 1960s, Americans in massive numbers began to join less, trust less, give less, and schmooze more" (p. 4). Trust is a community builder that generates social capital. As a resource for journey takers, trust can be replenished as a life-affirming catalyst (or depleted) along the way.

There is a "calling," then, with respect to Campbell's (1972/1993, 2008) identification of life journey stages, regarding trust-building for leaders and in challenging and complex times. Tschannen-Moran (2004) notes about trust in contemporary times,

> Trust poses a special challenge for school leaders because trust is so vital for schools to fulfill their fundamental mission of educating students to be productive citizens. Yet trust seems ever more difficult to achieve and maintain in the complex and rapidly changing world of the twenty-first century. (p. xi)

Because many people's world is socially fragmented, they live and work alone and feel emotionally disconnected. Thus,

> understanding the nature and meaning of trust in schools has taken on added urgency and importance. School leaders need to better understand the dynamics of trust in order to reap benefits for greater student achievement, as well as improved organizational adaptability and productivity. (Tschannen-Moran, 2004, p. xii)

According to Warren Bennis (1997), American management pioneer of the contemporary field of leadership studies, trust is a valuable asset for leaders.

In our changing world where we lack the types of social contracts we used to have with neighbors and coworkers, we build trust by having confidence in other people who have confidence in us. We want to be able to see evidence of competence and trustworthiness (Putnam & Feldstein, 2003).

Trust also depends on openness. Bennis (1997) declared that "control-and-command type" leaders fail to build trust. Another important strategy he identified for building trust is "deep listening": "It's the most powerful dynamic of human interaction when people feel they're being heard. Listening doesn't mean agreeing, but it does mean having the empathetic reach to understand another" (p. 75). Deep listening is a fundamental part of *cultural dialogue* for enacting social justice leadership, as described later in this chapter.

During the interviews, participants responded to what they perceived to be conditions for deep listening. After we reiterated the instructions for the session, we listened, only talking when initiating the movement from one interview prompt to another. They all opened up, making and sharing personal connections with the images.

Afterward they commented that the creative imaginative process they had engaged in was unusual for them, not only within the context of their school environments but also more generally in their lives. They also confided that they were accustomed to functioning at a superficial, more automated level of performance as leaders and that the interview had probed their interior selves in ways unfamiliar to them.

This exercise demonstrates that virtual strangers can build trust simply by ensuring conditions of safety that allow for letting go of the leadership persona of control. Supporting risk-taking through opportunities or discoveries respectful of the whole person propels an individual's journey. Having the space to express emotion supports engagement through deep listening. At a different scale, interpersonal trust can be developed within communities of leaders and followers.

Trust—and the building of it—is the leadership challenge of today. Interpersonal trust decreases cynicism, isolation, and conflict and increases optimism, connectedness, and conflict management. This kind of forward momentum is very much needed during times of uncertainty and change. Characteristics of trustworthy leaders include integrity, reliability, fairness, caring, openness, competence, and loyalty (Bennis, 1997; Duignan, 2012; Tschannen-Moran, 2004). The same can likely be said of cultures of trust wherein leaders and followers experience mutuality.

Organizational actions and policies that promote a culture of trust include investing in colleagues, promoting open communication, behaving in an ethical and socially responsible manner, and providing a measure of job security. Trust enables "organizational functioning"; without trust, a "school is likely to experience the overheated friction of conflict as well as a lack of progress toward its admirable goals" (Tschannen-Moran, 2004, p. xi).

We continue to build on these concepts from educational leadership research to emphasize them all from the social justice leadership lens. As English et al. (2012) describes in their portrait of socially just leaders for today and tomorrow, such leaders have a moral compass, the core principles of which are that (1) everyone has an equal right to the same liberty, and that (2) social and economic inequities need to be redressed, with the goal of preventing the perpetuation of systemic disadvantages.

A moral compass inspires leaders to take up such causes as poverty in their school communities (Mullen & Kealy, 2012). These leaders also examine inequities in opportunities and resources, as an example, and carefully discern which populations are at a disadvantage and why. They work closely with their teams to buffer students from academic and social failure while generating opportunities for lifelong success. Multiple journeys will intersect as community members become initiated as social justice advocates who take up the call, entering and departing at different entry points.

It has long been the case that more resources are channeled into high-achieving schools and students; systemic inequalities like this limit leaders' sphere of influence in, for example, disadvantaged school settings. Heroic actions of leadership reveal a broad spectrum of possibilities such as increasing educational opportunities for children and adults living in poverty and dealing with health and social disparities for children and adults.

Let's remember, though, that educational leaders "do not influence broad social realities, such as the tax structure of the state or the bankruptcy issues relative to housing or transportation needs" (English et al., 2012, p. 59).

When we put everything on leaders to change schools, we single them out. A target, they end up looking incompetent, unjust even, when they are expected to succeed by their hand alone. Communities stand by, watching. Politicians get let off the hook. So do taxpayers and for-profit corporations. Recessionary times have had a devastating effect on struggling schools, which makes advocacy for social justice even more arduous than before, as well as pressing.

There can be no real improvements in school performance without recognition that schools don't control all of the variables. Some variables such as poverty and class, in addition to the tax structure as mentioned, are linked to larger issues in the overall societal milieu (Mullen & Kealy, 2012). This predicament is the stuff for "heroism" in leadership that extends to policy-making circles.

Benefits of Building Trust for Leaders

Trust helps buffer an organization and make it resilient. Building on Bennis's (1997) ideas of trust and reading trust through a social justice lens, trust is an intangible asset that builds social capital. Social capital promotes cooperation, commitment, effort, improvement, and communication, all of which can help an organization survive and people grow their potential as human beings.

Socially just action depends on the building of trust through integrity, exhibiting basic honesty and moral character. A person of character can be trusted to do what is right even when there is no controlling authority. Their actions are congruent with the values and principles they espouse—they are guided by internal standards.

Such leaders are fair, and being fair means making unbiased decisions and not taking advantage of people. However, being considered fair also requires managing others' perceptions. In order to be perceived as fair, a leader should make standards clear and take the time to explain decision-making processes.

These leaders are also compassionate. Rationality is over-sold to us from the time we are children, when we are scolded for crying, for example. We should not ignore our emotions. We should not be put down for expressing them, and we should not be doing this to others. The most trustworthy leaders are those we can talk to about our worries and frustrations, and reveal what is in our hearts, because they care. And they listen.

Compassionate leaders are activists who do more than listen—they take action. But impervious leaders show no interest in hearing about others' concerns, and we do not trust or feel close to them. They treat others like disposable resources, and followers only pretend to follow. "Followers" will not go above and beyond the call of duty for such leaders and will even try to push them out by starting negative whispering campaigns, obstructing work flow, or other actions.

Socially just leaders exhibit openness. Trustworthy leaders keep confidences, but they are not in possession of harmful secrets or vital information and do not have hidden agendas. Open information-sharing involves a reciprocity: in such a culture, people will not withhold valuable information from leaders and followers will not resist opening up to leaders.

Competence is also essential to this picture. Trustworthy leaders perform their roles competently. Followers do not put their faith in incompetent leaders, even if those leaders are fair and caring.

You can't be socially just and not be loyal. Trustworthy leaders show through their actions that they are willing to protect and defend their followers when they make mistakes or during times of crisis. This kind of trust is particularly important during times of innovation and change because of inherent risks.

Again, we go beyond caring to emphasize the crucial role of compassion. Compassion is a catalyst not only for enabling all the aforementioned dispositions and behaviors but also for transforming environments into places that are fair, equitable, stimulating, creative, and mission-driven. You can see how important it is to have a high level of trust throughout an organization.

Based on case studies of leaders (Tschannen-Moran, 2004) and surveys on trust and collaboration by teachers (Tschannen-Moran, 2001), important discoveries have been made. It was found that school leaders who are trusted make profound changes but not too quickly, and that trust is essential for creating a school climate that nurtures collaborative relationships. Leaders foster relationships, propel vision, and align operational functions. They can lose trust by confronting conflict too soon or by avoiding conflict: "Benign neglect" perpetuates low morale and disillusion, allowing problems to fester (Tschannen-Moran, 2004, p. 4).

Caring, compassionate leaders accept or recognize the call to action that requires making uncomfortable decisions. Prickly personnel matters come to mind. We contend that social justice leaders who accept the call to action use core principles to guide their decision-making, such as ensuring that the rights of all people in their school community are considered in a fair and equitable manner (English et al., 2012).

What breeds mistrust are leadership actions that in addition to being neglectful of social justice issues, such as dynamics of poverty, unfairness, and inequity, support bureaucratic orientations of leadership. As established, leaders build trust by demonstrating "benevolence, reliability, competence, honesty, and openness" (Tschannen-Moran, 2001, p. 314).

To reiterate, leaders who are trusted do not exploit others for their own gain and they accept responsibility instead of deflecting blame. And they are authentic. Authenticity means sticking to the facts about people and situations by not distorting the truth. But wisdom in leadership recognizes that facts are limiting; human beings are multifaceted and your truth is someone else's lie. So we simulate truth-like opportunities and interventions, such as search committees, for interpreting as fully as possible someone's values, actions, and performances, which ironically evokes ambivalence (as discussed in chapter 3).

Principals who understand such complexities propel trusting climates by fostering "full collaboration" with teachers (Tschannen-Moran, 2001, p. 310). Leaders collaborate by allowing for shared problem-solving and by trusting that followers (e.g., teachers) contribute to organizational goals. Of course this means that overarching goals and shared values need to be established for stakeholders to have buy-in, and the same holds for parents and other groups.

How the leader goes about creating this culture will determine whether trust is developed and alliances are built across the entire body politic. A goal is to avoid ignoring the whole of one's group in favor of a few; selective attention isolates members of a community and can exacerbate frustration and mistrust. Alleviate frustration. Build widespread trust.

THE HUMAN CONDITION AND DIALOGUE BEYOND DIFFERENCE

It can be argued that the playing field for building trust as a leader and, more importantly, a community requires us to immerse ourselves in tensions associated with our own identity. When we think beyond our individual differences while still respecting them, we shift our leadership orientation by

> taking a broader, more ecumenical, and even more optimistic view of human identities and relations—a view that not only accepts difference and conflict based on clashing sectional identities, but also recognizes affinities and discerns conversations *across* these allegedly impermeable boundaries of identity, which embody and express a broader sense of humanity that goes beyond our dis-similarities. (Cannadine, 2013, p. 6)

Princeton University history professor David Cannadine (2013) wrote about the limitations of being wedded to difference and particular identities, such as religion, nationality, class, gender, or race, which then produces the narrative that one identity is more important than another.

Cannadine endorses the search for a view of the human condition that is not partial, pessimistic, and paranoid. Give sufficient attention to how people actually live out their lives and seek understanding of what they have in common. His stance is an alternative to the traditional discourse that separates people or types (e.g., socioeconomic classes) from one another.

Cultural dialogue brings pivotal tensions to light. Dialoguing with those who are different from ourselves—or are perceived to be—is also a strategy for building trust. Russian philosopher Mikhail Bakhtin (1895–1975) wrote that cultural discourse is inevitably partial and incomplete; while a communicative necessity—for it speaks to life and living and the human condition—it involves taking risks that may or may not succeed (as cited in Morson & Emerson, 1990).

The cultural dialogic orientation toward interaction between any individuals or groups, such as school leaders and their teams, highlights the importance of relationships. Shields (2004) believes that relationship-building is vital to transforming through cultural dialogue. Cultural dialogue involves interpersonal trust and risk-taking toward this goal. Social justice agendas can be abruptly circumvented, forced to take a backseat to school tests or any other competing agenda (Mullen et al., 2014; Shields, 2004). Trust-building suffers when leaders occupy mentally resistant fortresses that seal off broad possibilities for humanity captured by, for example, artistry in social justice leadership.

We can see from the educational leadership courses we teach in which aspiring leaders engage in the artistry of inventing/reinventing themselves that this is a steep climb. In their schools, they are expected to demonstrate a narrow-minded praxis with respect to test performance, making identity development and justice advocacy seem distracting. They are expected to build trust around an insular praxis that itself engenders mistrust among educators. This place of tension permeates the daily work of practicing leaders. It makes the journey toward wisdom hard to enact.

Pushing from the other direction, teachers and young people alike have expressed concern about deficit thinking. They have felt stigmatized by characterizations of their schools and neighborhoods as poor, underserved, and less than affluent schools (Shields, 2004). Stigmatizations deplete goodwill, let alone the capacity for entrusting schools to educate children for life in a global society. How can we expect school stakeholders to trust leaders and researchers if they do not trust the representations we create of them?

Relationally experienced dialogue with school constituents, whether teachers, leaders, youth, or parents, repositions praxis—it becomes two-way learning. Shoho, Merchant, and Lugg (2011) assert that it is the school's responsibility "to engage school leaders in a meaningful dialogue on social justice issues" (p. 37).

Schools of education in universities also have responsibility to encourage and create trusting dialogue with and on behalf of school practitioners and other stakeholders. A goal is to enlarge the sphere of responsibility that prepares educators so that school practitioners can feel more efficacious about leading and participating in difficult conversations.

Complicated dialogue is challenging for many reasons, including the fact that it is "central to the task of educational leadership" and is associated with "a way of being" (Shields, 2004, p. 115). Temple and Ylitalo (2009) also imagine universities as "places of possibility" and thus seek to involve their higher education populations "in social and cultural change" by using critical dialogue to surface "underlying assumptions about cultural and ethnic diversity" (p. 278).

The triad of trust concept has the potential to support the human enterprise of schooling. At the level of praxis, a bureaucratic orientation toward educational leadership is refuted. Instead, the primacy of a trusting orientation overtakes it through leadership demonstrations that are compassionate, have integrity, and are wise. Cultural dialogue is one strategy that channels trust-building for socially just leaders.

Key Concepts

Compassion. This emotion involves deep sympathy as well as an action component to move an individual toward doing something about a person or a condition. When it is situational, it may mean that conditions are unjust or unfair for the individual embedded in the situation.

Cultural dialogue. This form of interpersonal trust involves risk-taking. Dialoguing with others who are different from ourselves and/or perceived to be is a strategy for building trust. Cultural dialogue provokes answers that are particular and incomplete. The process is mutually educative and involves discovery and self-actualization or personal transformation (see Morson & Emerson, 1990). Relationship-building is a vital part of transformative cultural dialogue (Shields, 2004).

Emotion. Emotion refers to "feelings, moods, affect, and well-being" (Boekaerts, 2011, p. 412). Emotions have meaning interpersonally, culturally, and organizationally, and the experience and/or expression of them influences decision-making and social group experiences, including the degree of a group's readiness for social change (Blackmore, 2009).

People connect through emotions, primarily anger, disgust, fear, sadness, surprise, and joy. Emotions generate "action readiness" that sends warning signals, preparing the body for action (Boekaerts, 2011, p. 413; see also Zimmerman & Schunk, 2011). Emotional connection can produce positive synergy or negative energy, causing people, who are not robots, to feel and act differently (Harding & Pribram, 2004).

Integrity. Trustworthy actions on the part of people (e.g., leaders) who make ideas and information available to all parties are said to have integrity. Such "data availability" or full disclosure ensures no secrets. This is the basis for what Bottery (2003) has called *identificatory trust,* which is itself "a deep-rooted interpersonal relationship characterized by a complex intertwining of personal thoughts, feeling and values" (p. 253). Cultural or organizational integrity generates trustworthiness and trust among stakeholders. Integrity creates the conditions for schools and other organizations to wisely resist corruption (Duignan, 2012; Tschannen-Moran, 2004).

Leadership for social justice. As defined by Dantley and Tillman (2006), "Leadership for social justice investigates and poses solutions for issues that generate and reproduce societal inequities" (p. 17; for additional ideas, see also Mullen, 2008; Mullen, Harris, Pryor, & Browne-Ferrigno, 2008). As described in this chapter, it is difficult for educators to investigate social inequities within their school without trust (Savage & English, 2013).

Trust. There are three levels of trust, which is based on predictability, dependability, and faith (Rempel, Holmes, & Zanna, 1985). The first level develops when "individuals rely on established or predictable behavior and emotional responses in a given environment" (Schmidt, 2010, p. 50).

When the actions of individuals or organizations are viewed not only as predictable but also as responsive to people, there is a medium level of trust. That is the second level.

The third level is the highest; it "reflects an emotional security in others or institutions where there is a belief that individuals or institutions will keep their promises in their efforts to be responsive to the needs of stakeholders" (Schmidt, 2010, p. 51).

Wisdom. Leaders who are wise exhibit integrity and compassion, and they use this leadership quality to help them make difficult decisions while guiding others (Lawrence, 2011). Wise leaders help people maintain perspective and they challenge them to grow, regardless of economic, social, and other barriers. Such leaders also create cultures of trust where meaningfulness matters and hope is present. People experience higher levels of cohesion and morale around wise leaders as well as a greater capacity for taking action despite anxieties and fears (Tschannen-Moran, 2004), and despite behavioral obstacles such as poor motivation.

We now move to chapter 5 and conclude with a calling to our readership.

Chapter Five

Revealing Relevance for Practice, Preparation, and Research

We are not the first to use Joseph Campbell's work in educational leadership, but we believe we are the first to test it empirically with visual data. In this final chapter we explain why this is unique and what it means for practice, preparation, and research.

In exploring the relevance of our study, although we separate it into three realms, in reality they are all part of one whole. As coauthors, we have all been professors in higher education institutions involved with the preparation of researchers and practitioners. Our backgrounds, academic preparation, and practitioner credentials as coauthors total 108 years of experience that spans academia, pre K–12 school settings, community colleges, and other settings. We value artistry in leadership and learning. We have published scholarship in arts-based educational research and on the use of visual data in research, and we have taught visual information design and production.

As we tried to make sense of what we had learned from this study we considered its impact for leadership practice, preparation, and research. To make meaning of the data, we drew on parallels in theoretical and empirical work by different scholars in various fields, including educational leadership. Some of the most relevant research that connected with our themes is cited in this book.

Perhaps the first obstacle we encountered in explaining the relevance of our work was getting out of the shadow of the theory-practice gap. First, we take issue with the traditional view of this concept, which is that somehow all that "theory" taught in classes at the university is worthless in guiding school leaders in the day-to-day business of educating children and youth. We think that this represents only a half-truth that should be confronted.

MAKING WHOLE THE THEORY-PRACTICE GAP

Theories are simply narratives, and all practice is at one time based only on decisions and actions carried out following a narrative or theory. When narratives become normative (prescriptive) they serve as the basis for informing and guiding professional practice. Over time, those narratives become lost, and practitioners carry out their practices without the knowledge of the theories on which they rest. In this case, they are just practicing practice. This is one sort of theory-practice gap. It might be called a "theory-less" practice gap.

Philosopher Lakatos (1999), who introduced the concept of research program in his scientific studies, identified two types of perspectives on theories in relationship to practice. Some theories follow practice; for example, when practitioners work in their applied settings they innovate and experiment without knowing exactly what the outcomes might be because the theories in use do not include the actions being taken.

While we do this in education, medical practice is famous for these situations, when doctors discover a cure for a problem but can't explain why it works. History has shown that unless medical practitioners can attach practice to theory, the theoretical perspective is not accepted (see LeFanu, 1999).

Lakatos (1999) calls this case one of a "regressive research program," meaning that the theories in use no longer inform, guide, or predict results. The opposite case occurs when theory leads practice. It not only accurately describes practice, but also anticipates problems and predicts outcomes. This kind of research program is "progressive." Here the "theory-practice" gap exists because practice is far behind theory.

We believe our research points to the need to restore the human and emotional dimensions of leadership to a rightful place in practice, preparation, and research. We believe that our current theories of leadership will not become progressive, as Lakatos described, until we include the full human being in leadership standards, university courses, and research. We are not the only ones who hold such a position, however.

TOWARD CHANGING THE DISCOURSE OF EDUCATIONAL LEADERSHIP

Typically the concept of discourse refers to all forms of communication, written and oral, that comprise a discipline such as educational leadership. Foucault (1972) called this concept a discursive formation that must satisfy four criteria: it must refer to the same objective; share in the same level of modality; function in a system of conceptual organization; and, finally, share similar theories and themes.

We were not the first to find Campbell's universal journey metaphor valuable for educational leaders (see, e.g., Brown & Moffett, 1999); however, we can find no other study that applies Campbell's work in the same kind of empirical setting. Our results challenge the dominant current discursive formation of our field. The part of it that is groundbreaking is the use of visual data.

Unfortunately, in educational leadership the rational choice (economic) models that dominate our discourse have been regressive for some time. Not only that, but they have also inhibited the development of theories that deal with the human and emotional side of leadership, which we believe our study underscores. Take French sociologist Pierre Bourdieu (1985), who fiercely opposed rational choice theory. His critique of this theory centers on the idea that it is grounded in a misunderstanding of the social world and how social agents operate within "relatively indeterminate" (p. 728) spaces.

Instead, as we argue elsewhere, possibility, the unknown, and mystery are significant. "Possibility and the unknown are givens" in the social domain of leadership wherein "leaders seize the opportunity to elicit and transform their world by inviting and producing plural perspectives that introduce an 'element of play, of uncertainty' in their decision-making" (English et al., 2012, pp. 33–34). Our participants did not respond as though they saw schools as limited social spaces, and they did acknowledge that conflicting forces were at work in education that control imaginative dynamics within multidimensional social spaces.

Bourdieu's (1985) contention was that social agents operate according to an implicit practical logic and bodily dispositions. In other words, people do not continuously calculate according to explicit rational and economic criteria. We are not machines! This is where emotions come in, because social agents (e.g., school leaders) feel their way as they go and experience emotions that they may or may not express—or even recognize—as they interact with others, carry out their work, and change their cultures.

As Bourdieu (e.g., 1985) explains across his many works, relational research practice and theory-building in organizational (e.g., leadership) studies are two directions scholars need to go, and we underscore these ideas in this book by making leadership humane. And by making the full human being the centerpiece of our selected framework of the universal life journey.

We posit that our current discursive formations must be expanded in these two directions—relational research practice and theory-building in leadership studies—if our theories are to have a chance of becoming progressive. If there can be such a thing as a bottom line in educational discourse, theories of leadership need to embrace, explain, and forecast a rich array of human interactions in the co-construction of leadership practice in educational settings.

That will not happen unless and until we are able to include the full human being in our studies and teachings. To do that we will have to include what we know about leadership from the arts and humanities (see Ehrich & English, 2013). How relational research practice and theory-building in leadership studies can support this endeavor need to be considered by other scholars and practitioners.

MIRROR MIRROR ON THE WALL, WHO AM I?

What about the mystery of leadership? Our identity as leaders and human beings—who we really are at the core of our being—remains largely unknown during adult maturity and even at the end of life. It is, to quote former prime minister of the United Kingdom Winston Churchill, "a riddle, wrapped in a mystery, inside an enigma" (Churchill Society, 2014).

Consider our original artwork titled *The Mystery of Identity* (figure 5.1). The conundrum of identity may be represented by mirrors shown in two paintings, Pablo Picasso's *Girl before a Mirror*[1] and Rene Magritte's *Not to Be Reproduced*.[2] As shown, we collapsed the images from these paintings into a single visual image (figure 5.1).

In Picasso's cubist work, the painter's mistress is ambiguously portrayed, perhaps to show her "day-self and her night-self, both her tranquility and her vitality, but also the transition from an innocent girl to a worldly woman aware of her own sexuality" (Museum of Modern Art, 1999/2004, p. 161). The image of a body composed of many moving parts—triangle and circles, and back, side, and front views—suggests a shape-shifting world. The younger girl is reaching out toward the older woman, who seems anxious; it is as if the girl is trying to unite her different selves.

In our artwork, we used the image of the mirror from Magritte's painting but not the male figure; instead, we used the female figure from Picasso's painting. Both paintings use mirrors, and we have simply swapped the figures.

For our artwork we did what Magritte did—we took the girl standing in front of the mirror and duplicated the figure exactly as her reflection, thereby turning Picasso's cubist work into surrealism. Magritte was obsessed with the idea of representation (recall the painting of a smoking pipe and the caption, "This is not a pipe," he painted below it; the same with his depiction of a huge apple and his printed words, also scrolled in French, "This is not an apple"). Magritte's point is that the viewer shouldn't take representation literally.

Representation is a lot like identity. The most commonplace sense of our own identity, even more so than with photographs, is standing in front of a mirror. The thing is that what you see in a mirror is not what other people

Figure 5.1. The Mystery of Identity

see. The reflection is a bogus reflection of identity. In our artwork we combined the two to produce a visual pun.

We used Picasso's female figure in the same way that Magritte used a male figure in his painting, in that the reflection in the mirror is the same image as the figure, an exact duplication. Melding the Picasso and Magritte paintings into one image plays with the concept of identity while also commenting on the impenetrable task of authentically knowing oneself.

Who we really are is a mystery. We spend our lives trying to grasp who we are, only to eventually realize that this is an elusive exercise at best. We have dedicated an entire book to the subject of seeking to understand how leaders make sense what they see in powerful photographs and perceptions they have of life as a journey—which is itself a metaphoric reflection of reality and thus a representation of it.

Mirrors give us a false impression of who we are, just as photographs do. This is doubly confounding. In our original artwork there is a play on identity: Do we ever really know who we are? The image of ourselves is reversed in the mirror; photographic versions are not identical either. But emotions are real, regardless, and they are powerful agents of our own truth-telling.

RELEVANCE FOR PRACTICE

The implications of our research for practice are that they counter the managerial and instrumental models being pushed by neoliberals in their tyrannical efforts to "reform" schools (English, 2014; Mullen, English, Brindley, Ehrich, & Samier, 2013; Mullen, Samier, Brindley, English, & Carr, 2013). The model of trust that is part compassion, part integrity, and part wisdom is not being advanced as the antidote to any serious problem that schools are facing. What we are offering is not a medical remedy for the problems of schools but rather a framework for propelling artistry and social justice leadership.

Neoliberal reforms are not concerned with matters of social justice— inequalities in the larger society that impact school communities. They are concerned with promoting "market values" of those attitudes; Schmidt (2009) argues, "Ultimately, these values will shape the definition of leadership at the expense of leaders' emotions as they are subverted from social justice goals of promoting democracy, critical citizenship, and basic human rights" (p. 148).

We know this sounds bleak, but just ask any school leader about the messages they are receiving about "control and predictable output" and how this makes them feel when they have been charged with fostering "innovative thinking, creative thinking, strategizing, and problem solving" (Tienken & Orlich, 2013, p. 39). The current policy context, especially as "foreshadowed in the Common Core Standards movement to nationalize curriculum standards and testing and the Race to the Top (RTTT) program," is being viewed as a form of "collective punishment" (Tienken & Orlich, 2013, p. 39).

From this perspective, rational choice theory is driving school change and is fueled by behaviorism, which applauds control and predictable outcomes and outputs, as well as the science of control. In this world, the defenseless suffer even more.

Remember the bullies from your school days and how they changed the feeling/tone of the school or neighborhood to one of reigning terror? Now scale up this scenario. What do you get? Bigger, more powerful bullies targeting schools.

Further, consider the anti-teachers'-union rhetoric advanced by the reformers. It is not one in which trust, collaboration, and transparency can exist. To many reformers of current practice in schools the main agenda is about efficiency, standardization, and profiting as more and more public schools are privatized with charters, vouchers, and other forms of public school takeover. This trend is occurring even though data clearly indicate that these alternative schools, at least as a collective, underserve special-needs populations and (re)segregate children and youth based on race and class (see, e.g., Banchero & Porter, 2012; Mullen, Samier, Brindley, English, & Carr, 2013; Tienken & Orlich, 2013).

The kind of schools that are agents of social justice advocacy are those where leaders foster what Crawford (2009) called "a climate of genuine emotion" (p. 192). Without such a climate the creation of healthy work environments, fueled by trust and integrity, are not likely to exist. Schools become toxic when social agents are motivated by extreme selfishness, avarice, competition, jealousy, secrecy, and fear. Blackmore (2009) associated this type of climate with "fear of disposability," characterized by high levels of emotional insecurity where workers are disposed of after use or fear that they will be.

Such insecurity increases when threats become real, as in when coworkers are given a limited shelf life. Generationally speaking, baby boomers and many others yearn for stability in the form of "a sustained life narrative"; they "take pride being good at something specific," "value the experiences they've lived through," and desire "a rightful and secure position in society" (Sennett, 2006, pp. 5, 24).

We see these troubling forces at play in leaders' lives, but we also see imagination, connection, and resiliency in leaders. With respect to our participants, we believe that the resilient themes of Campbell's work in universal mythology are present in the educational leaders. Their emotional responses to visual data indicate to us that they were connected to those themes.

The behaviorists out there have not stamped out our souls, at least not yet. There was room for mystery and the unknown in the participants' sensemaking about the images. Ponderous moments. Facial expressions. A tear. Thus we hold that, as Heilbrunn (1996) observes, "the mystery of leadership touches on some of the more vexing philosophical questions about human existence, which theorists ignore only at the risk of ultimate irrelevance" (p. 11).

RELEVANCE FOR PREPARATION

Too much of our coursework in the academy is based on rational, economic, and business models that only include part of what is required to effectively lead schools. Our programs are founded on only one-half of what it takes to be a leader. From this perspective, we are only preparing leaders to handle a limited number of the real tasks they will face. In many cases they are not being prepared to create environments for their stakeholders that are trusting and that build on compassion, integrity, and wisdom, which are crucial for generating cohesion and fueling advocacy (see English & Papa, 2010).

School leaders cannot function in a public place that is quintessentially a moral intersection of culture, tradition, and ideals for a future without a foundation of faith. Faith in an undefined future that is largely ambiguous and nonquantifiable does not fit the for-profit mindset that is being advanced as the antidote for some underperforming schools (English et al., 2012). Faith is not a subject of any higher education curriculum we know—faith begins where social science ends.

One example of how unprepared one of the coauthors was in being a superintendent of schools involves the death of a student. A child had been killed outside the superintendent's office when he walked into the path of a truck while listening to rock music through a headset. The school nurse had not seen that kind of head wound since World War II. The superintendent was called on to express condolences to the immigrant parents for whom the son was the only child. The superintendent prepared remarks and delivered them at the funeral, and wrote a column for the high school newspaper.

Nothing had prepared the superintendent for such an emotionally charged assignment or human loss. Preparation relative to the whole human being had been missing from traditional training. Acts of compassion magnified in this community and became a very large and visible dimension of leadership. The death of a student can be traumatic, anxiety-provoking, and life changing. The role of the leader in such times is to be compassionate by, for example, offering reassurances where there is fear and suffering, and taking action to foster conditions that uproot negative emotions (Gardner, 1995). Like the superintendent, we may not always be aware when we are calling on the life journey framework as a guide for moving a community from loss to acceptance to renewal, and from an individual focus to a communal one.

Medawar (1984) indicated that the issues that the superintendent in this vignette confronted belong to an arena that "science cannot answer and that no conceivable advance of science would empower it to answer" (p. 129). This is the power of the leadership identity journey that Joseph Campbell advanced. It is a narrative that deals with the ultimate issues in human life. Bolton and English (2009) put it this way:

The meaning of this dilemma for leaders is that if the stories they are required to tell to become empowered by followers are not scientific questions that can be addressed by social science methods in preparation programmes, then in what context can it be said that they are prepared to lead if the world does not conform to the assumption of such methods? (p. 129)

How do we prepare aspiring leaders to be wise? How do we help them tap their own wisdom and nurture it in the course of their daily work? In our coursework, how might we present the concept of wisdom in such a way that our students of leadership will internalize it and infuse wisdom into their praxis as leaders of school communities?

Based on the results of our study, we would want all leaders of schools to model the importance of maintaining perspective when feeling challenged or overwhelmed, to learn from their mistakes and misadventures, and to become more intelligent by creating meaning out of circumstances. The wisdom of Gandhi belongs to the wisdom of all aspiring and practicing leaders—it is not privy to some and not others. It is not an elitist concept or a limited resource.

Leaders who are taught to be caring but not compassionate will not rise to the level of competency and effectiveness that we would want for them. Leaders who do not consistently expect integrity from themselves and others will not gain the respect of their followers, and trust that is built or inherited will be broken. Leaders who learn the concepts of wisdom from our leadership courses, implicitly evidenced in such forms as social justice theory and action, need guidance in confronting inequities in society (and in their own school communities) and proactively pursuing wisdom and modeling its tenets for others.

We do not see the word *wisdom* showing up in higher education course titles or research in educational leadership. As leadership faculty, we have yet to mindfully seize on the value of this bedrock concept of enlightenment in our field of study and practice. We can no longer leave it to the purview of programs of religion to teach about wisdom.

It is time we recognize wisdom as a core leadership concept—and component of trust along with compassion and integrity—that will in turn support the construction of social justice as the breakthrough "invention" of leadership faculty. With trust as the engine of this vision, we can with deeper conviction invest faith and hope in the capacities of aspiring leaders to perform heroic actions.

RELEVANCE FOR RESEARCH

The dominant discursive formation in educational leadership has been rational choice theory rooted in economics. It is complemented by research strategies that are embedded in theories of organization from sociology, structuralism, and behaviorism. For the most part, these perspectives eliminate the full human being from all decision-making; the so-called nonrational aspects are not perceived to be relevant to a "scientific study" of leadership. We have tried to underscore the importance of changing the research practices and the models on which they are based.

Future research directions include building on cognitive aesthetics, relational research practice, and theory-building in organizational (e.g., educational) studies (Bourdieu, 1985). Cognitive aesthetics, as we have discussed, takes into account the emotional side of decision-making in research conducted on educational leadership (Brown, 1977). Relational research practice involves a research encounter where we find ourselves emotionally moved, touched, and awed by the spontaneous connections others make and the way they make us feel.

In this book, we have tried to capture something of our research encounters, experienced as thickly populated microcosms involving multiple subjectivities, sparks of insight, and a range of emotional expressions. When researchers open themselves to such creative uncertainties and to whatever might emerge in that intersubjective space with participants, entirely new life worlds can present themselves. We feel privileged to have had this experience. It took courage for the school leaders to sit with uncertainty and unknowing. It took receptivity to be open to what emerged in the "now" of the embodied encounter.

We chose not to engage in our own storytelling with the research participants; however, researchers may find it valuable to try this and see whether involving mutual self-disclosure might be useful and even help stimulate authenticity in storytelling.

As we intertwine with another in a research encounter, we may find ourselves surprised, touched, and awed by the connections we make and discover. The encounter may involve co-transferences in that the selves of one person elicit those of the other. Self-disclosure is part and parcel of meaning-making, and whether this is handled one-way, as we chose to do, or two-way, is the purview of the researcher and the goals of the project.

Researching the topics of trust and social justice is a natural place to build on our work. We have presented what we refer to as the triad of trust framework (see chapter 4). As previously discussed, its components are compassion, integrity, and wisdom, and at the core of leadership for social justice is trust (see figure 4.1).

Researchers can explore the dynamics of trust as linked to human emotion. From the social justice leadership lens, what evidence is there that compassionate, action-oriented caring individuals are indeed leading schools and are being prepared to do so in our leadership programs? To what extent are leaders simply caring, as in empathetic to others, but not action oriented? This is a concern, as what we need in the world are leaders fully committed to causes that promote advocacy for socially just schools and educational systems.

In this book we ask whether educational leaders experience a breathtaking, all-consuming, transformative leadership journey, and whether they see themselves on a journey of growth and development, as humans and as leaders.

We posit that if educational leaders intuit that their lives and/or professional development are on a path, implications need to be considered for leadership, conducting research, and preparing future educational leaders.

These are the overarching research questions that guided our study. A primary source of inspiration we tapped is Joseph Campbell's description of the university mythic pattern. We think that researchers can build on our suppositions to expand the applicability of our findings to the experiences of leaders, both in their work and in their lives.

What we saw in our results is that school leaders interpret their inner and outer worlds and they create frameworks to make sense of stimuli they encounter. They do it every day. When confronted with life, death, and loss, they bring discrepant events into a narrative that goes beyond schooling.

All of the leaders were able to identify with the concept of the human condition and tell a story in relation to a selected photograph. The same was true for the trials in life theme, the concept of human transformation or change, and the notion of a person crossing an important threshold in life, as well as leadership in general.

Our respondents represented the universal leadership journey using archetypes similar to Campbell's. We saw them struggle with the ambiguity and complexity inherent in sensemaking and with their own emotions, which they sometimes expressed. A common face of humanity emerged from their responses.

The Journey's Phases: Departure, Initiation, and Return

Educational researchers can borrow from this open-ended template to involve respondents in their studies.

Departure: Adventure Prior to the Quest

What call have you accepted (or rejected) in your work as an educational leader that turned out to be a significant decision? What feelings, thoughts, or struggles did you experience during this phase of your leadership journey?

Initiation: (Mis)adventures along the Way

While on the journey, what experiences did you encounter? Who or what helped, challenged, or blocked you? What trials did you undergo? These take the form of a series of tests, tasks, or ordeals that the person must undergo to begin the transformation.

Return: Return Home with Knowledge and Powers

What did you experience upon your return home to the ordinary world? What new insight did you gain from your journey? What wisdom did you come to and have you had the opportunity to integrate the wisdom from your quest into your work or being? Have you taken action by sharing your wisdom with personal networks or even the rest of the world?

Key Concepts

Discursive formation. According to Sawyer (2002), Foucault used this term to replace the concept of scientific discipline. It refers to all forms of expression, written and oral, that comprise a series of statements. Lacan (1968) believed that such statements formed the basis of the construction of self.

Progressive research program. This is a situation where the theory in use is ahead of practice and predicts what effects practice will have if implemented. It is a different kind of "gap," one that posits that "theory-in-use" is a powerful and useful narrative.

Rational choice theory. This narrative posits that human action and behavior should be based on logic and reason and should screen out emotions as irrational and negative.

Regressive research program. Based on the ideas of Imre Lakatos (1999), a regressive research program is one in which theory is behind practice. This is the traditional view of the "theory-practice" gap.

Theory-practice gap. As traditionally understood, the theory-practice gap refers to the inability of theory to influence and guide leadership practice and, by way of implication, the false premise that educational leadership professors are unable to influence and guide aspiring leaders of schools. Belief in the theory-practice gap lies behind the contemporary movement in some urban areas in which school districts form their own leadership academies instead of having their future leaders prepared in university programs.

NOTES

1. To view Picasso's painting online, go to: www.moma.org/collection/object.php?object_id=78311.

2. For Magritte's painting, visit www.wikipaintings.org/en/rene-magritte/not-to-be-reproduced-1937.

Coda

Our purpose in this final section is to clarify and extend our own thinking, hopefully for the benefit of other researchers. Perhaps readers will want to engage in similar explorations with creative stimuli, such as interpretive visual data. Or perhaps readers will pursue an inquiry that moves beyond the usual sort of survey research or interviewing protocols in qualitative research.

Our study was bounded by the realities of securing Institutional Review Board (IRB) approval for conducting leadership research from our respective locations within U.S. institutions of higher education. Over the years, the coauthors have read many research proposals and given and attended many presentations where educational research has been vetted.

We have observed that the research "backstory" is often not given, despite the continually changing body of work that constitutes educational research today. Thus, we strive to make a unique contribution to the larger discourse on research in leadership studies by bringing to the foreground the research backstory of our study, which in and of itself may be a unique contribution to artistry in leadership studies. This backstory is extended to include a series of vignettes on our topic produced by educators in an Internet context.

We have been fortunate to be in a position of leading national and international agendas in our roles as executive officers of two national professorial organizations, the University Council for Educational Administration (UCEA) and its older counterpart the National Council of Professors of Educational Administration (NCPEA). Yet we still have a strong desire to conduct scholarship that opens up educational leaders to the process of making meaning of universal ideas relative to their life worlds, particularly by creative and evocative means that spotlight the interpretive use of visual data.

ON CAMPBELL'S *HERO WITH A THOUSAND FACES*: A THEORY, METAPHOR, OR ART?

We regarded Campbell's (2008) work on universal mythology not as a formal scientific theory to be tested (or subjected to falsification as in philosopher Popper's [1965, 1968] approach) in the usual sort of the way theories are conceptualized with propositions that can be subjected to verification. Campbell's universal mythology lens may be more of a unifying metaphor than a theory, a kind of overriding script or a codex, if you will. It was not our intention to "prove" (or "disprove") in the traditional or classical sense whether Campbell's premises have legitimacy.

Rather, we sought to learn whether Campbell's metaphor and its junctures have the potential to resonate with contemporary educational leaders of schools. We wondered if practicing leaders could be stimulated—provoked, even—with photographs to interpret their meaning in a manner consistent with or parallel to Campbell's lens. Our work was motivated not only by our curiosity but also by our desire to engage in creative scholarly work that potentially brings artistry to leadership.

The fact that our respondents' interpretations assumed patterns is a testimony both to the confluence of image, culture, and context in which they work and to the universality of Campbell's notion. We were also interested to know if what Campbell called a "living mythology" was present in the understandings of our educational leaders and we were affirmed in this quest. We all are living some kind of mythology—it may not be in the sense of classical Greek myths, but these nonetheless have at their core Campbell's narrative constructs of departure, initiation, and return.

Humans create mythology to find comfort in and make sense of a world that appears indifferent to our struggles—even to our very existence. Nothing is more quintessentially human than to try to create solace and warmth in what appears to be an unforgiving and cruel environment. And the comfort needed occurs around birth, marriage, celebration, love, and success. Even in distress we are reminded of hope and renewal, as in the life of a newborn or just in the presence of a bright star in an otherwise dark sky. No matter where humans are, the culture and country of residence, these occurrences mark our existence—they are universal.

Another way of viewing *The Hero with a Thousand Faces* is an aesthetic object, a work of art that is itself a reason to exist. As such it represents what Bourdieu (1977) calls "pure practice without theory" (pp. 1–2)—it is not explainable by a transcendent code. We tended not to accept this perspective, but it was considered.

In her role as past president of the NCPEA, Carol Mullen had the opportunity to post a blog at the organization's website. For it, she briefly described the concepts from Campbell's mythology and the overarching ideas of departure, initiation, and return.[1] Seven bloggers responded to whether educational leaders see themselves on a journey that has the potential for personal transformation, as well as implications for leadership, conducting research, and preparing future educational leaders.

In a nutshell, the bloggers wrote that they considered the concept of the journey important and revelatory, and that the "connection" between professional practice and the journey motif was a powerful one for them. Quoting verbatim from two of the blog entries:

> I am a believer that a student should exit my class as a different student than the one who started the journey. It is my desire that the student is more aware, more thoughtful, and more willing to lead. As a leader, I learned from many others along the way, and I am not the person I was. It is the difference between "being" and "becoming." I am still in the process of becoming, and as I experience that process, I hope to affect change in the world around me.

> I see a variation of the authors' ideas in the transformation of some of my doctoral students as they make their way through the leadership program. They all bring biases and goals they want to accomplish as a leader. In many cases those biases and goals are somewhat parochial and derive from their experiences in the place they work. In some instances candidates come with romantic views of education and are unaware of the neoliberal forces conspiring against public education.

For the two professors quoted, graduate courses in educational leadership themselves represent a journey and an opportunity for students to undertake transformative learning and emerge better able "to affect change in the world" around them. They learn about the importance of interrogating their own "biases and goals" and those they carry into their higher learning from their school districts.

And they become introspective as learning-oriented leaders. This happens as they study how power and wealth, concentrated by transnational corporations and global elite groups, negatively affect disenfranchised groups and public education. (For a study of the complex picture involving the neoliberal agenda and its influence on public schooling, see Mullen, English, Brindley, Ehrich, & Samier, 2013; Mullen, Samier, Brindley, English, & Carr, 2013.)

The journey phases Campbell introduced were viewed as relevant, with the initiation phase considered equivalent to people's "internal struggle" around such issues as values and biases, and an evocation toward consciousness-raising through educative acts, such as data assessment and analysis.

> I equate Initiation to the internal struggle some candidates face when confronted with evidence and data that challenges their biases and raises their awareness that they have additional responsibilities beyond that of "running" a building. They also have the responsibility to advocate for the public school

system, democracy's incubator. They have a responsibility to understand the big picture in terms of policy and politics, and get involved in "setting the record straight" at the local, state, and/or national levels.

You can see the transformation from Pollyanna to leader in the candidates who are willing to examine their biases and seek evidence. They change as people. These types of students often say that they can no longer look at the world the same way.

In the return phase, the leader makes a difference by applying what has been learned in graduate studies to educating those around him or her:

> I think the Return phase can be seen when those candidates who transformed go out and do things differently in the places they work. They also begin to spread what they learned to others who might still be stuck in the romantic realm of schooling.

The value placed on the study of existence as related to education and the process of "becoming" was reflected in several comments, most clearly in the following:

> I find the connection between professional leadership practice and one's existential journey wholly refreshing. As an emerging scholar of existential philosophy and philosophy of education, I believe that a renewed focus on the individual—from student, to educator, to administrator—is necessary to understanding education as human endeavor. I also embrace the concept of "becoming." At all levels within the realm of education, the individual can choose "becoming" as an ongoing possibility for personal enrichment and for contributing to the social good.

For a few of the bloggers, the blog was itself deemed revelatory: "A true revelation! This journey is one that every educational leader travels through, but at vastly varying levels of cognition about the journey and varying outcomes at journey's end."

This same blogger wrote about the personal journey taken, and in some detail. The entire passage is worth including as it focuses on the acceptance of a call in the form of changing one's career from school leader to educational leadership professor. Also, the story references the trials along the way for which the traveler was not prepared and the emotional hurdles associated with the internal struggle, notably loneliness, as well as the emotional benefits, such as excitement.

The boon comes with gratification from teaching advanced courses, from experiencing networking opportunities, and from leading an enriched life. Realizations come from persevering with the process of evolving in the course of one's leadership journey.

As a young K–12 educational leader in the ordinary classroom and AP ranks, I received an opportunity (Call) to enter the educational leadership doctoral program, an unknown monstrosity, a scary chance to leave K–12 tenure, paychecks, and stability all for a temporary shot at being graduate assistant with the temptation of obtaining strange new college teaching powers. I reluctantly accepted the call and began the strange journey through a whole new world with many tough trails and life straining tribulations, for most of which I was wholly not prepared! Often times I felt alone, even though faculty and staff were, so called, "available."

After being repeatedly told often that "what doesn't kill you, makes you stronger," I dug deep and somehow, someway, persevered. Actually, this huge challenge motivated me in a strange way. After sinking at first, somehow not only did I survive, but thrived in the rush and excitement. Teaching undergraduates and the [odd] doctoral class was truly my "boon." I was on the top of the world. If I could just keep up somehow and triumph through the rest of the courses and keep up with grading undergraduate work, I could return to K–12 with three letters behind my name [i.e., EdD] and doors would fly open for me, hopefully, or would they?

The latter thoughts and [the steps of Campbell's journey framework] coupled with the former motivation completely transformed me somehow! I couldn't go back. I didn't want to go back. This was too exciting and I had my eyes opened to much more that I could accomplish. Most of my colleagues went back and thrived. I chose the different path and am enjoying the benefits. I am still teaching college and loving it! This life-changing journey has given me new insights, wisdom, and amazing networking opportunities.

I think the further one is away from the journey, the clearer it all becomes. It is hard to see while you are in it. The best wisdom I can offer is summed in one word, "perseverance," apparently a strange phenomenon to so many in the newest generations.

In his transition from school leadership to graduate school as a student, the departure was marked by a feeling of reluctance. For another blogger, currently an experienced professor in higher education who had also transitioned from the public school system as a leader, the point of initiation was marked with a feeling of discomfort. Feeling restless, perhaps seeking to extend her reach, she took a new path, as narrated by her in some detail.

Departure phase. I entered public education as a teacher and loved being a teacher. About 5 years later, I had the opportunity to help start a private school where I taught for a few more years, became principal of the elementary school and then became the headmaster. By this time, the school which had started with fewer than 100 students, now had 1,000 students in grades 1–12. I loved this job and could have done it for many years, but after nearly 20 years in this setting, I became uncomfortable. Within me there was a desire to "do more." Why would I want to leave what I loved? Why wasn't I satisfied? Based on this experience, I would say that my Departure began with Discomfort.

Initiation phase. So, I acknowledged this discomfort and acted upon it to leave the K–12 school setting and entered higher education as an assistant professor in educational leadership. As I embarked upon Initiation in this new setting, my learning adventures have been far more than I ever anticipated. I have worked with school leaders from all over the United States and beyond. In my quest for "more" I've developed friendships that have extended my personal and professional borders. I've had mentors who were younger and older, but wise in their understanding of the many facets of leadership. Some of these mentors were already established as leaders in the field, others were students from whom I have learned so much about leadership and more importantly about myself as a human being.

Return phase. When I critically reflect upon the Return phase of my journey, there have been many important acquisitions. One of the important learnings has been that leadership learning is reciprocal. I lead and you learn about leading; you lead and I learn about leading. We grow from our experiences with others when we allow ourselves the freedom to accept and acknowledge our weaknesses and emphasize our strengths. Thus, the leadership journey is about being transparent to others, ever becoming who we desire to be, and accepting the weaknesses and strengths of others as a natural part of our shared and respected common humanity. In this way, we learn to celebrate the journey—not as a way to lead others, but as a way to lead *with* others in creating a better world today and for those nameless leaders who will journey later.

Restlessness, as just described, to do something more or different in one's professional life is one motivator for taking the leadership journey. In the initiation phase, the departing school leader began learning anew as an adventure and developed many educative friendships.

As a professor of many years, the insights described by this same individual for the return phase revolve around the idea that leadership relies on the learning of all team members and that "leadership learning is reciprocal." From the perspective of this phase, the leadership journey is viewed as an experience of "common humanity," characterized by transparency in relationships, an acceptance of people in their fullest sense, and the experience of active, ongoing learning as a leader who leads with others.

The bloggers wrote about other qualities and skills—such as innovation, management, and implementation—needed by those embarking on a personally transformative leadership journey. In one case, the scenario described involves the creation of programs and policies.

Leadership is a journey needing skills and qualities each step along the road. The initiation of a project—the creation of programs and policies—that get people energized for action tends to be the easy part. The day-to-day support and attention to maintenance details that make the program or policy work is as important a quality of leadership as the skills and qualities that brought about the initiation of a project. Carrying out the program by the people who do the implementation is where the real success lies. [American film director]

Woody Allen said, "80% of success is just showing up." I'd paraphrase Mr. Allen and say, "80% of a successful program is just showing up when the work needs to be done."

Regarding the call to a challenge seemingly greater than one's self-perceived abilities, the subsequent trials, and the needed aid that often comes from an unexpected source, one blogger was reminded of the book *The Scottish Himalayan Expedition* (Murray & Anderson, 1951) and mountaineer W. H. Murray's observation about commitment:

> Concerning all acts of initiative (and creation), there is one elementary truth, the ignorance of which kills countless ideas and splendid plans: that the moment one definitely commits oneself, then Providence moves too. All sorts of things occur to help one that would never otherwise have occurred. A whole stream of events issues from the decision, raising in one's favour all manner of unforeseen incidents and meetings and material assistance, which no man could have dreamt would have come his way. (cited in Pressfield, 2002, p. 122)

About Emotionality and Its Place in Leadership Practice and Research

About the study reported in this book, as researchers we were taken aback by the strong emotional responses of our respondents to the visual images shown in the photographs. They were expressive, both verbally and nonverbally, and they each went on a journey of the imagination as they pondered the photographs and responded to the associations evoked by them.

We have previously conducted studies predicated on very structured, logical, and typical interview questions. But in all of those studies, we had not encountered the emotive, often visceral, responses of leaders grappling with nonscientific questions relating to life, death, and identity. It was profound as well as humbling for us to be in the presence of leaders as they struggled to put words to deep emotions, especially in an educational research context.

After all, we were asking about a human being's life journey, which is filled with trials, hopefully some triumphs, and the inevitable defeats of leaders that Ackerman and Maslin-Ostrowski (2002) described as "wounding." The vividness and evocative emotions displayed struck chords within us as well. We began to see how important the emotional side of leadership is in sustaining and giving meaning to the stresses, strains, and struggles in schools today.

It is not that the coresearchers had not experienced the emotional dimensions of leadership, but at that time we did not have any way to connect those experiences with a larger narrative. In answer to the query if our research was not some sort of self-fulfilling prophecy on our part, we would disagree. We neither expected nor anticipated what our respondents would say or how they would respond. We were quite amazed when we ourselves felt moved and when in our data analyses their responses became convergent.

In actuality, we really didn't know how or if our respondents would find anything of interest, let alone of significance, in the images we shared. We were aware of taking a risk, knowing we could come up empty handed, and we were prepared for any kind of response, even being shrugged off. And we knew it was a possibility that our respondents might not find anything meaningful about the images we showed them. It would have been acceptable, too, if we had found that there was nothing especially common in their interpretations of the photographs.

Considering Visual Data, Images, Context, Culture, and Narrative

Campbell's most basic outline of human life as portrayed in mythology over time was our verbal prompt for visual images. It is clear to us as researchers that context, culture, linguistic syntax, and prevalent narratives of childhood as identified by Howard Gardner (1995) were somehow at work in our interviewees' reactions. While the images chosen were not the process of random selection, neither could it be argued that leadership is a random activity. The meaning of visual images involves a complex process of social construction, in leadership the social activity of co-construction between leaders and followers.

It seems entirely plausible that any number of theoretical lenses could have been used as verbal prompts. For example, we could have staked out a lens using Maslow's Hierarchy of Needs[2] (2013)—a contested theory of human motivation that focuses on the stages of growth in humans (e.g., physiological, security, social, esteem, and self-actualizing needs) with respect to the patterns that human motivations move through—and asked our interviewees to sort the visual images by which of the five human needs they would represent. But this set of verbal prompts would not be the same as the ones employed in our study of the universal leadership journey.

Visual data are multilayered (see, e.g., Mullen, 1999, for research focused on pencil drawings on personal existential topics created by female inmates) and as occurred in our study were not categorically exclusive. In some cases very evocative photographs were selected to represent more than one juncture in Campbell's leadership journey. (The junctures, as outlined in table 1.1, are human condition, trials in life, human triumph, human transformation, human crossing, and, we added, leadership.)

Photographs as shifting phenomena categorically overlap. This underscores Sontag's (1977) point that part of what informs the meaning-making of photographs is the verbal context in which they are framed. Similarly, our respondents chose some of the same photographs, both individually and collectively, to capture phases of the life journey, which may have occurred in concert with or as a result of their verbal telling or our verbal prompts, or both.

Another view of our subject matter involves Bourdieu's (1980) concept of habitus. Habitus, a complex idea, represents what a human being learns unconsciously about values and social action. This forms a kind of practical knowledge of "sense" within a particular field—sometimes called "the rules of the game"—and contains a "certain purposefulness without conscious purpose, an intentionality without deliberate intention, obeying" (p. 66).

Our respondents were occupants in a specific field: education. They brought to the research task a conscious application in addition to their individual habitus; one's habitus is expressed unconsciously and in relation to stimuli. The importance of this factor is hard to calculate in any precise terms, but Lane (2006) explains that

> the body [is] not merely a blank screen, passively registering external stimuli as empiricism would have it, rather it exerted a grip on the world; it was actively engaged in the world, tending towards the world and seeking to make sense of it, accumulating practical knowledge about the world. (p. 44)

This "practical knowledge," which actively engages in sensemaking, Lane (2006) attests, "constitute[s] a series of incorporated 'sedimentations' of habitual ways of acting, viewing and evaluating the world" (p. 44). Further, these thoughts and behaviors are not indicative of "deliberative judgment" but rather "affect, desire and taste" (p. 44).

Undoubtedly, the similarities in culture, context, and social class strata in which our leaders work was also a factor in the convergence in their photographic interpretations, but there is no way to calculate how much this contributed to the results. Clearly, our respondents were not merely passive recipients of the visual images we shared—they actively engaged in sensemaking about the world.

About the Nature of Theory

When we argue for a restoration of the so-called nonrational aspects of leadership to be included in future research, we are aware that the way theory is conceptualized often precludes the nonrational from being examined insomuch as it is difficult to quantify in the typical kind of survey methodologies that are the staple of graduate studies. Using what amounts to psychosocial questions and responses would make many graduate students uncomfortable as well as their faculty program committees and respondents, not to mention the kinds of issues that would be raised by most IRB oversight committees.

We would like to see emotional kinds of research used more frequently to probe the full scope of educational leadership in schools. We confess that our knowledge of most leadership preparation programs, including those of our current employment, would not be very conducive to learning or employing them. The difficulty itself is testimony to how dominant the rational/logical models have become and why we think their prevalence has given us so very little new information about educational leadership.

According to English and Papa (2010), about 53 percent of all dissertation research (completed from between 2006 and 2008) employs qualitative approaches. While there has been an increase of qualitative research methods in educational leadership, the theories behind these studies remain largely in the thrall of logical/rational economic models, methods, and expectations. We need to include a much fuller range of human leadership and it's not just a matter of enlarging existing theories but of creating a whole new range and type of theory.

These theories would be characterized by comprehensiveness, fluidity and complexity, predictability as probabilities in context, and leading practice rather than following it. We briefly explain each of these theories:

a) *Comprehensiveness*—Logic and emotion are portrayed as interactive, functioning in a holistic manner with a variety of combinations possible as dictated by context. Our stipulation of this condition is based on our own experience as educational administrators in K–12 and higher education settings. We are aware that our minds and hearts play off one another and that in some situations the heart has a logic all its own. We need a theory that can entertain that phenomenon and not simply add emotion to current logical/rational situations.

b) *Fluidity and complexity*—We don't need new approaches that reduce the complexity and fluidity of leadership to skills, attributes, and ultimately checklists. This approach robotizes what is essentially human performance in situ. Leadership is essentially an art form when it is operationalized, not static or lifeless. One way of thinking about this is to consider examining leadership as dramatized scenarios of an improvisational nature.

c) *Predictability as probabilities in context*—Leadership is not a random activity. It is bound by culture, context, and the use of signs and symbols, especially language. Instead of being characterized by the false finality of numbers, we see leadership as characterized by ranges of probable responses contingent on such circumstances as the risk involved, confidence, transparency, and trust. We see it as a multidimensional, multilayered judgmental and personalized set of interactions that are highly contextualized.

d) *Leading practice rather than following it*—Leadership research should be progressive. As noted by Lakatos (1999), a progressive research program should explain not only more than what is currently being done, but also what is possible within ranges of probabilities where we can predict certain responses and outcomes.

Currently, most of our theories in leadership simply describe and partially explain, but none predict with any confidence, even with ranges of possibilities, what actions will lead to what outcomes. The complexities and realities of leading schools exceed the capacity of the theories to even come close to capturing them with any precision or reliability.

And we confess that the nature of both precision and reliability may have to be radically changed because they are remnants of a social science paradigm that is woefully inadequate to provide us with any but the most rudimentary and partial understanding of effective leadership.

We want you to know that we view the research based on powerful photographs reported in this book as work in progress, an initial, exploratory probe into the emotional world of educational leaders. There is much more to learn and do. It is our hope that our work will inspire our readers to continue exploring.

NOTES

1. The blog, titled "Leadership Journeys: Paths to Professional Practice," was posted at the NCPEA website blog titled *Talking Points: News, Views, and Opinions on Leadership in Education*. Between November and December 2013 seven bloggers responded. Identifying as "anonymous," they reflected a pool of invitees who are educators, professors of educational leadership, as well as doctoral students of leadership studies and educational philosophy. For the blog post, visit http://ncpeaprofessor.org/wp-admin/&reauth=1/2013/11/19/leadership-journeys-paths-to-professional-practice.

2. 1943 was the original version, as cited in the references.

References

Ackerman, R. H., & Maslin-Ostrowski, P. (2002). *The wounded leader: How real leadership emerges in times of crisis.* San Francisco: Jossey-Bass.

Alinsky, S. (1971). *Rules for radicals: A practical primer for realistic radicals.* New York: Vintage Books.

Andrews, E. A. (1854). *Copious and critical Latin-English lexicon.* New York: Harper & Brothers.

Attenborough, R. (1982). *The words of Gandhi.* New York: New Market Press.

Banchero, S., & Porter, C. (2012, June 20). Fewer disabled go to charter schools. *Wall Street Journal*, p. A2.

Banks, M. (2001). Visual anthropology: Image, object and interpretation. In J. Prosser (Ed.), *Image-based research: A sourcebook for qualitative researchers* (pp. 9–23). London: RoutledgeFalmer.

Barber, J. (1985). *The presidential character: Predicting performance in the white house* (3rd ed.). Englewood Cliffs, NJ: Prentice-Hall.

Barthes, C. (1980). *Camera lucida: Reflections on photography.* (R. Howards, Trans.) London: Jonathan Cape.

Barthes, R. (1977). *Image, music, text.* (S. Heath, Trans.) London: Grafton Books.

Beck, L. G. (1999). Metaphors of educational community: An analysis of the images that reflect and influence scholarship and practice. *Educational Administration Quarterly, 35*(1), 13–45.

Becker, H. (1978). Do photographs tell the truth? *Afterimage, 5,* 9–13.

Benenate, B. (1997). *In the heart of the world: Thoughts, stories & prayers Mother Teresa.* Novato, CA: New World Library.

Bennis, W. (1989). *On becoming a leader.* Cambridge, MA: Perseus Books.

———. (1997). *Managing people is like herding cats.* Provo, UT: Executive Excellence.

Berger, J. (1972). *Ways of seeing.* Harmondsworth, London: Penguin.

Bergman, I. (1990). *Images: My life in film.* New York: Arcade.

Blackmore, J. (1999). *Troubling women: Feminism, leadership and educational change.* Buckingham, UK: Open University Press.

———. (2009). Measures of hope and despair: Emotionality, politics, and education. In E. A. Samier & M. Schmidt (Eds.), *Emotional dimensions of educational administration and leadership* (pp. 109–124). London: Routledge.

Bloom, C. M., & Erlandson, D. A. (2003). African American women principals in urban schools: Realities, (re)constructions, and resolutions. *Educational Administration Quarterly, 39*(3), 339–369.

Blount, J. (2005). *Fit to teach: Same sex desire, gender, and school work in the twentieth century.* Albany, NY: SUNY Press.

Boekaerts, M. (2011). Emotions, emotion regulation, and self-regulation of learning. In B. Zimmerman & D. H. Schunk (Eds.), *Handbook of self-regulation of learning and performance* (pp. 408–425). New York: Routledge.

Bogotch, I., & Shields, C. M. (Eds.). (2014). *International handbook of educational leadership and social (in)justice* (volumes 1 and 2). New York: Springer.

Bolton, C. L., & English, F. W. (2009). My head and my heart: De-constructing the historical/ hysterical binary that conceals and reveals emotion in educational leadership. In E. Samier & M. Schmidt (Eds.), *Emotional dimensions of educational administration and leadership* (pp. 125–142). London: Routledge.

———. (2010a). De-constructing the logic/emotion binary in educational leadership preparation and practice. *Journal of Educational Administration, 48*(5), 561–578.

———. (2010b). Exploring the dynamics of work-place trust, personal agency, and administrative heuristics. In E. A. Samier & M. Schmidt (Eds.), *Trust and betrayal in educational administration and leadership* (pp. 29–42). London, UK: Routledge.

Bottery, M. (2003). The management and mismanagement of trust. *Educational Management and Administration, 31*(3), 245–261.

Bourdieu, P. (1977). *Outline of a theory of practice.* (R. Nice, Trans.) New York: Cambridge University Press.

———. (1980). *The logic of practice.* (R. Nice, Trans.) Cambridge, UK: Polity Press.

———. (1984). *Distinction: A social critique of the judgment of taste.* (R. Nice, Trans.) Cambridge: Harvard University Press.

———. (1985). The social space and the genesis of groups. *Theory and Society, 14*, 723–744.

Bredeson, P. V. (1985). An analysis of the metaphorical perspectives of school principals. *Educational Administration Quarterly, 21*(1), 29–50.

Brown, J. L., & Moffett, C. A. (1999). *The hero's journey: How educators can transform schools and improve learning.* Alexandria, VA: ASCD.

Brown, R. H. (1977). *A poetic for sociology: Toward a logic of discovery for the human sciences.* Cambridge: Cambridge University Press.

Campbell, J. (1972/1993). *Myths to live by.* New York: Viking Press.

———. (1990). *Transformations of myth through time.* New York: Harper and Row.

———. (2008). *The hero with a thousand faces* (3rd ed.). Princeton, NJ: Princeton University Press.

Cannadine, D. (2013). *The undivided past: Humanity beyond our differences.* New York: Knopf.

Cartier-Bresson, H. (1999). *The mind's eye.* New York: Aperture.

Chalfen, R. (2001). Interpreting family photography as pictorial communication. In J. Prosser (Ed.), *Image-based research: A sourcebook for qualitative researchers* (pp. 214–234). London: Routledge.

Chhuon, V., Gilkey, E., Gonzalez, M., Daly, A., & Chrispeels, J. (2008). The little district that could: The process of building district-school trust. *Educational Administration Quarterly, 44*(2), 248–291.

Churchill Society. (2014). Retrieved from www.churchill-society-london.org.uk/RusnEnig.html.

Crawford, M. (2009). The leader and the team: Emotional context in educational leadership. In E. A. Samier & M. Schmidt (Eds.), *Emotional dimensions of educational administration and leadership* (pp. 186–197). London: Routledge.

Crossan, J. D. (1975). *The dark interval: Towards a theology of story.* Niles, IL: Argus Communications.

———. (1994). *Jesus: A revolutionary biography.* San Francisco: HarperCollins.

Dantley, M. E., & Tillman, L. C. (2006). Social justice and moral transformative leadership. In C. Marshall & M. Oliva (Eds.), *Leadership for social justice: Making revolutions in education* (pp. 16–30). Boston: Pearson.

Davis, S. H. (2004). The myth of the rational decision making: A framework for applying and enhancing heuristic and intuitive decision making by school leaders. *Journal of School Leadership, 14*(6), 621–652.

Derrida, J. (1993). *Aporias.* (T. Dutoit, Trans.) Stanford, CA: Stanford University Press.

Drucker, P. F. (1974). *Management: Tasks, responsibilities, practices.* New York: Harper & Row.

Duignan, P. (2012). *Educational leadership: Together creating ethical learning environments* (2nd ed.). Cambridge, UK: Cambridge University Press.

Ehrich, L. C., & English, F. W. (2013). Leadership as dance: A consideration of the applicability of the "mother" of all arts as the basis for establishing connoisseurship. *International Journal of Leadership in Education, 16*(4), 454–481.

Eisner, E. W. (2002). *The arts and the creation of mind.* New Haven, CT: Yale University Press.

Ekman, P., & Friesen, W. V. (2003). *Unmasking the face: A guide to recognizing emotions from facial clues.* Cambridge, MA: Malor Books.

Ekman, P., & Rosenberg, E. L. (2005). *What the face reveals: Basic and applied studies of spontaneous expression using the Facial Action Coding System (FACS).* Oxford, UK: Oxford University Press.

English, F. W. (1988). The utility of the camera in qualitative inquiry. *Educational Researcher, 17*(4), 8–15.

———. (2002). The point of scientificity, the fall of the epistemological dominos, and the end of the field of educational administration. *Studies in Philosophy and Education, 21*(2), 109–136.

———. (2006). Preface: A new conception of the knowledge base of a profession. In F. W. English (Ed.), *Encyclopedia of educational leadership and admin is tration* (pp. xxxv–xxxvi). Thousand Oaks, CA: SAGE.

———. (2007). The NRC's *scientific research in education*: It isn't even wrong. In F. W. English & G. Furman (Eds.), *Research and educational leadership* (pp. 1–38). Lanham, MD: Rowman & Littlefield Education.

———. (2008a). *Anatomy of professional practice: Promising research perspectives on educational leadership.* Lanham, MD: Rowman & Littlefield Education.

———. (2008b). *The art of educational leadership: Balancing performance and accountability.* Thousand Oaks, CA: SAGE.

———. (2014). *Educational leadership in the age of greed: A requiem for res publica.* Ypsilanti, MI: NCPEA.

English, F. W., & Bolton, C. L. (2008). An exploration of administrative heuristics in the United States and the United Kingdom. *Journal of School Leadership, 18*(1), 96–119.

English, F. W., & Papa, R. (2010). *Restoring human agency to educational administration: Status and strategies.* Lancaster, PA: Pro>Active.

English, F. W., Papa, R., Mullen, C. A., & Creighton, T. (2012). *Educational leadership at 2050: Conjectures, challenges and promises.* Lanham, MD: Rowman & Littlefield Education.

Erikson, E. H. (1969). *Gandhi's truth: On the origins of militant nonviolence.* New York: Norton.

Feyerabend, P. (1993). *Against method.* London: Verso.

Fischer, L. (1950). *The life of Mahatma Gandhi.* New York: Harper & Brothers.

Foster, W. (1986). *The reconstruction of leadership.* Victoria, NSW: Deakin University Press.

Foucault, M. (1972). *The archaeology of knowledge and the discourse on language.* New York: Pantheon Books.

Frick, D. M. (2004). *Robert K. Greenleaf: A life of servant leadership.* San Francisco: Berrett-Koehler.

Funk, R. W., Hoover, R. W., & the Jesus Seminar (1993). *The five gospels: What did Jesus really say? The search for the authentic words of Jesus.* New York: Macmillan.

Gandhi, M. (1948). *Gandhi's autobiography: The story of my experiments with truth.* (M. Desai, Trans.) Washington, DC: Public Affairs Press.

Gandhi, R. (2008). *Gandhi: The man, his people, and the empire.* Berkeley: University of California Press.

Gardner, H. (1995). *Leading minds: An anatomy of leadership.* New York: Basic Books.

———. (1997). *Extraordinary minds.* New York: Basic Books.

Gardner, J. (1963). *Self-renewal.* New York: Harper & Row.

———. (1969). *No easy victories.* New York: Harper Colophon Books.

Gardner, P. L. (1987). Measuring ambivalence to science. *Journal of Research in Science Teaching, 24*(3), 241–247.

Gates, H. L., Jr., & West, C. (2000). *The African-American century: How black Americans have shaped our country.* New York: Simon & Schuster.

Goldberg, V. (1987). *Margaret Bourke-White: A biography.* Reading, MA: Addison-Wesley.

Goldhagen, D. J. (1996). *Hitler's willing executioners: Ordinary Germans and the Holocaust.* New York: Knoph.

Goleman, D. (1998). *Working with emotional intelligence.* New York: Bantam.

Gorn, E. J. (2001a). *Mother Jones: The most dangerous woman in America.* New York: Hill & Wang.

———. (2001b). *The history of Mother Jones.* [Mother Jones and the Foundation for National Progress]. Retrieved from www.motherjones.com/about/what-mother-jones/our-history.

Greenfield, T. B., & Ribbons, P. (1993). *Greenfield on educational administration.* London: Routledge.

Hackman, D. G., & McCarthy, M. M. (2011). *At a crossroads: The educational leadership professoriate in the 21st century.* Charlotte, NC: Information Age.

Halling, S., Leifer, M., & Rowe, J. O. (2006). Emergence of the dialogal approach: Forgiving another. In C. T. Fischer (Ed.), *Qualitative research methods for psychologists: Introduction through empirical studies* (pp. 247–278). San Diego: Elsevier.

Hamilton, G. (2008). Mythos and mental illness: Psychopathy, fantasy, and contemporary moral life. *Journal of Medical Humanities, 29*, 231–242.

Harding, J., & Pribram, D. (2004). Losing our cool? Following Williams and Grossberg on Emotion. *Cultural Studies, 18*(6), 27–42.

Heilbrunn, J. (1996). Can leadership be studied? In P. S. Temes (Ed.), *Teaching leadership: Essays in theory and practice* (pp. 1–12). New York: Peter Lang.

Henley, P. (1998). Film-making and ethnographic research. In J. Prosser (Ed.), *Image-based research: A sourcebook for qualitative researchers* (pp. 42–59). London: RoutledgeFalmer.

Horwitt, S. D. (1989). *Let them call me rebel: Saul Alinsky, his life and legacy.* New York: Knopf.

Iyer, R. N. (1973/2000). *The moral and political thought of Mahatma Gandhi.* New York: Oxford University Press.

———. (Eds). (1993). *The essential writings of Mahatma Gandhi.* Delhi: Oxford University Press.

Jack, H. A. (Ed.) (1951/1979). *The wit and wisdom of Gandhi.* New York: Dover.

Jung, C. G. (1958). *The undiscovered self.* New York: Mentor Books.

———. (1967). *Symbols of transformation.* (R. F. C. Hull, Trans.) Princeton, NJ: Princeton University Press.

KetsdeVries, M. (1993). *Leaders, fools, and imposters.* San Francisco: Jossey-Bass.

Kouzes, J. M., & Posner, B. Z. (2002). *The leadership challenge.* San Francisco: Jossey-Bass.

Lacan, J. (1968). *The language of the self: The function of language in psychoanalysis.* Baltimore, MD: Johns Hopkins Press.

Lakatos, I. (1999). *The methodology of scientific research programmes.* Cambridge, UK: Cambridge University Press.

Lakoff, G., & Johnson, M. (1980). *Metaphors we live by.* Chicago: University of Chicago Press.

Lane, J. F. (2006). *Bourdieu's politics: Problems and possibilities.* London, UK: Routledge.

Larsen, S., & Larsen, R. (1991). *A fire in the mind: The life of Joseph Campbell.* New York: Doubleday.

Larue, G. A. (1975). *Ancient myth and modern man.* Englewood Cliffs, NJ: Prentice-Hall.

Lawrence, T. E. (2011). *Seven pillars of wisdom: A triumph: The complete 1922 text*. Blacksburg, VA: Wilder.

LeFanu, J. (1999). *The rise and fall of modern medicine*. New York: Carroll and Graf.

Lelyveld, J. (2011). *Great soul: Mahatma Gandhi and his struggle with India*. New York: Vintage.

Levi-Straus, C. (1967). *Structural anthropology*. New York: Doubleday.

Little, D. E. (1999). Philosophy of the social sciences. In R. Audi (Ed.), *The Cambridge dictionary of philosophy* (pp. 704–706). Cambridge, UK: Cambridge University Press.

Lortie, D. C. (1998). Teaching educational administration: Reflections on our craft. *Journal of Cases in Educational Leadership, 1*(1), 1–12. Retrieved from www.ucea.org/cases.

Louis, K. S. (2006). *Organizing for school change*. New York: Routledge.

Lumby, J., & Coleman, M. (2007). *Leadership and diversity: Challenging theory and practice in education*. London: SAGE.

Lumby, J., & English, F. W. (2009). From simplicism to complexity in leadership identity and preparation: Exploring the lineage and dark secrets. *International Journal of Leadership in Education, 12*(2), 95–114.

———. (2010). *Leadership as lunacy: And other metaphors for educational leadership*. Thousand Oaks, CA: Corwin.

Lupton, D. (1998). *The emotional self: A socio-cultural exploration*. Thousand Oaks, CA: SAGE.

March, J. G. (1984). How we talk and how we act: Administrative theory and administrative life. In T. J. Sergiovanni & J. E. Corbolly (Eds.), *Leadership and organizational culture* (pp. 18–35). Urbana: University of Illinois Press.

March, J. G., & Olson, J. P. (1976). *Ambiguity and choice in organizations*. Bergin, Norway: Universitetsforlaget.

Maslow, A. H. (2013). *Maslow's hierarchy of needs*. Eastford, CT: Martino Fine Books. [Original: Maslow, A. H. (1943). A theory of human motivation. *Psychological Review, 50*(4), 370–396.]

McGregor, D. (1960/2006). *The human side of enterprise*. New York: McGraw-Hill.

Medawar, P. (1984). *The limits of science*. Oxford, UK: Oxford University Press.

Merriam-Webster. (2003). *Merriam Webster's collegiate dictionary*. Springfield, MA: Author. Retrieved from www.merriam-webster.com/dictionary/compassion.

Miles, M., & Huberman, A. (1994). *Qualitative data analysis* (2nd ed.). Thousand Oaks, CA: SAGE.

Morris, D., Collett, P., Marsh, P., & O'Shaughnessy, M. (1979). *Gestures*. New York: Stein and Day.

Morson, G., & Emerson, C. (1990). *Mikhail Bakhtin: Creation of a prosaics*. Palo Alto, CA: Stanford University Press.

Mullen, C. A. (1999). Reaching inside out: Arts-based educational programming for incarcerated women. *Studies in Art Education, 40*(2), 143–161.

———. (2008). Democratically accountable leader/ship: A social justice perspective of educational quality and practice. *Teacher Education Quarterly, 35*(4), 137–153.

———. (2011). The paradox of change in public schooling and education leadership. In F. W. English (Ed.), *The Sage handbook of educational leadership: Advances in theory, research, and practice* (2nd ed., pp. 69–80). Thousand Oaks, CA: SAGE.

Mullen, C. A., English, F. W., Brindley, S., Ehrich, L. C., & Samier, E. A. (2013). Neoliberal Issues in Public Education issue. *Interchange: A Quarterly Review of Education, 43*(3) (part I) and *43*(4) (part II), 181–377 (two-volume issue).

Mullen, C. A., Greenlee, B. J., & Bruner, D. Y. (2005). Exploring the theory-practice relationship in educational leadership curriculum through metaphor. *International Journal of Teaching and Learning in Higher Education, 17*(1), 1–14. Retrieved from www.isetl.org/ijtlhe/pdf/IJTLHE17.pdf.

Mullen, C. A., Harris, S., Pryor, C. R., & Browne-Ferrigno, T. (2008). Democratically accountable leadership: Tensions, overlaps, and principles in action. *Journal of School Leadership, 18*(2), 224–248.

Mullen, C. A., & Kealy, W. A. (2012). Poverty in school communities. *Kappa Delta Pi Record, 49*(2), 70–77.

Mullen, C. A., & Robertson, K. (2014). *Shifting to fit: The politics of Black and White identity in school leadership.* Charlotte, NC: Information Age.

Mullen, C. A., Samier, E. A., Brindley, S., English, F. W., & Carr. N. K. (2013). An epistemic frame analysis of neoliberal culture and politics in the US, UK, and the UAE. *Interchange: A Quarterly Review of Education, 43*(3), 187–228.

Mullen, C. A., Young, J. K., & Harris, S. (2014). Cultural dialogue as social justice advocacy within and beyond university classrooms. In I. Bogotch & C. Shields (Eds.), *International handbook of educational leadership and social (in)justice* (pp. 1145–1168, volume 2). New York: Springer.

Murphy, J., & Forsyth, P. B. (1999). A decade of change: An overview. In J. Murphy & P. B. Forsyth (Eds.), *Educational administration: A decade of reform* (pp. 3–38). Thousand Oaks, CA: Corwin.

Murray, W. H., & Anderson, R. (1951). *The Scottish Himalayan expedition.* London: J. M. Dent & Sons.

Museum of Modern Art. (1999/2004). *MoMA highlights.* New York: Author.

Nieuwenhuizen, L., & Brooks, J. S. (2013). The assistant principal's duties, training, and challenges: From color-blind to a critical race perspective. In J. S. Brooks & N. Witherspoon Arnold (Eds.), *Antiracist school leadership: Toward equity in education for America's students* (pp. 185–209). Charlotte, NC: Information Age.

Nisbet, R. (1970). *History of the idea of progress.* New York: Basic Books.

Nguyen, T. (2010). *Language is a place of struggle: Great quotes by people of color.* Boston: Beacon.

Papa, R., English, F. W., Davidson, F., Culver, M. K., & Brown, R. (2013). *Contours of great leadership: The science, art, and wisdom of outstanding practice.* Charlotte, NC: Information Age.

Pattison, S. (1997). *The faith of the managers: When management becomes religion.* London: Cassell.

Pearson, C. S. (1991). *Awakening the heroes within: Twelve archetypes to help us find ourselves and transform our world.* New York: HarperCollins.

———. (1998). *The hero within: Six archetypes we live by.* New York: HarperCollins.

Peeters, B. (2013). *Derrida: A biography.* (A. Brown, Trans.) Cambridge, UK: Polity Press.

Popper, K. R. (1965). *Conjectures and refutations: The growth of scientific knowledge.* New York: Harper & Row.

———. (1968). *The logic of scientific discovery.* New York: Harper Torch Books.

Pressfield, S. (2002). *The war of art.* New York: Black Irish Entertainment LLC.

Preston, T. (2011). *A walk to the crossroads.* Bolivar, MO: Quiet Waters.

Price, M. (1994). *The photograph: A strange, confined space.* Stanford, CA: Stanford University Press.

Putnam, R. D., & Feldstein, L. M. (with Cohen, D.). (2003). *Better together! Restoring the American community.* New York: Simon & Schuster.

Quote DB. (2009). Albert Einstein. Retrieved from www.quotedb.com/quotes/2310.

Rempel, J. K., Holmes, J. G., & Zanna, M. P. (1985). Trust in close relationships. *Journal of Personality and Social Psychology, 49*(1), 93–112.

Ribbins, P. (2006). Aesthetics and art: Their place in the theory and practice of leadership in education. In E. Samier & R. Bates (Eds.), *Aesthetic dimensions of educational administration and leadership* (pp. 175–190). Oxon, UK: Routledge.

Roberts, J. (1998). *The art of interruption: Realism, photography and the everyday.* London: Cameraworks.

Robinson, J. A. (1981). Personal narratives reconsidered. *Journal of American Folklore, 94*, 58–85.

Rosen, C. (2013, October 16). The gadget and the bad Samaritan. *Wall Street Journal*, p. C3.

Rost, J. (1991). *Leadership for the twenty-first century.* New York: Praeger.

Samier, E. A., Bates, R. J., & Stanley, A. (2006). Foundations and history of the social aesthetic. In E. A. Samier & R. J. Bates (Eds.), *Aesthetic dimensions of educational administration and leadership* (pp. 3–17). Abingdon, Oxon, UK: Routledge.

Savage, L., & English, F. W. (2013). Unmasking social injustice in the classroom: The achievement gap and Bourdieu's cultural reproduction theory. In S. Harris & S. Edmonson (Eds.), *Critical social justice issues for school practitioners* (pp. 121–145). Ypsilanti, MI: NCPEA.

Sawyer, R. K. (2002). A discourse on discourse: An archeological history of an intellectual concept. *Cultural Studies, 16*(3), 433–456.

Schmidt, M. (2009). Accountability and the educational leader. Where does fear fit in? In E. A. Samier & M. Schmidt (Eds.), *Emotional dimensions of educational administration and leadership* (pp. 145–159). London: Routledge.

———. (2010). Educational trust: A critical component in the (de)cultivation of social capital in school districts. In E. A. Samier & M. Schmidt (Eds.), *Trust and betrayal in educational administration and leadership* (pp. 43–59). New York: Routledge.

Schweitzer, A. (1965). *The teaching of reverence for life.* New York: Holt, Rinehart and Winston.

Scott, D. (2003). (Ed.). *Curriculum studies: Major themes in education.* New York: Taylor & Francis.

Sennett, R. (2006). *The culture of new capitalism.* New Haven: Yale University.

Sergiovanni, T. J., & Corbolly, J. E. (Eds.) (1984). *Leadership and organizational culture.* Urbana: University of Illinois Press.

Shields, C. M. (2004). Dialogic leadership for social justice: Overcoming pathologies of silence. *Educational Administration Quarterly, 40*(1), 109–132.

Shields, C. M., & Mohan, E. J. (2008). High-quality education for all students: Putting social justice at its heart. *Teacher Development, 12*(4), 289–300.

Shipman, N. J., Queen, J. A., & Peel, H. A. (2007). *Transforming school leadership with ISLLC and ELCC.* Larchmont, NY: Eye on Education.

Shoho, A. R., Merchant, B. M., & Lugg, C. A. (2011). Social justice: Seeking a common language. In F. W. English (Ed.), *The SAGE handbook of educational leadership: Advances in theory, research, and practice* (2nd ed.) (pp. 36–54). Thousand Oaks, CA: SAGE.

Shweder, R. A. (1994). "You're not sick, you're just in love": Emotion as an interpretive system. In P. Ekman & R. J. Davidson (Eds.), *The nature of emotion: Fundamental questions* (pp. 32–44). New York: Oxford University Press.

Smith, M. L., Miller-Kahn, L., Heinecke, W., & Jarvis, P. (2004). *Political spectacle and the fate of American schools.* New York: Routledge.

Solomon-Godeau A. (1991). *Photography at the dock: Essays on photographic history, institutions and practices.* Minneapolis: University of Minnesota Press.

Sontag, S. (1977). *On photography.* New York: Farrar, Straus and Giroux.

Temple, J. B, & Ylitalo, J. (2009). Promoting inclusive (and dialogic) leadership in higher education institutions. *Tertiary Education and Management, 15*(3), 277–289. doi: http://dx.doi.org/10.1080/13583880903073024.

Tienken, C. H., & Orlich, D. C. (2013). *The school reform landscape: Fraud, myth, and lies.* Lanham, MD: Rowman & Littlefield Education.

Todd, S. (1997). *Learning desire.* London: Routledge.

Tooms, A. K., Lugg, C. A., & Bogotch, I. (2010). Rethinking the politics of "fit" and educational leadership. *Educational Administration Quarterly, 46*(1), 96–131.

Trachtenberg, A. (2007). *Lincoln's smile and other enigmas.* New York: Hill and Wang.

Tschannen-Moran, M. (2001). Collaboration and the need for trust. *Journal of Educational Administration, 39*(4), 308–331.

———. (2004). *Trust matters: Leadership for successful schools.* San Francisco: Jossey-Bass.

———. (2009). Fostering teacher professionalism in schools: The role of leadership orientation and trust. *Educational Administration Quarterly, 45*(2), 217–247.

Viall, P. (1989). *Managing as a performing art: New ideas for a world of chaotic change.* San Francisco: Jossey-Bass.

Weber, M. (1991/1922). *The sociology of religion.* Boston: Beacon.

Weick, K. E. (1995). *Sensemaking in organizations.* Thousand Oaks, CA: SAGE.

———. (1996). Fighting fires in educational administration. *Educational Administration Quarterly, 32*(4), 565–578.

Wells, L. (2005). *Photography: A critical introduction* (3rd ed.). London: Routledge.

Wolterstorff, N. P. (1999). Empiricism. In R. Audi (Ed.), *The Cambridge dictionary of philosophy* (2nd ed., pp. 262–263). New York: Cambridge University Press.

Ylimaki, R. M. (2006). Toward a new conceptualization of vision in the work of educational leaders: Cases of the visionary archetype. *Educational Administration Quarterly, 42*(4), 620–651.

Zaretsky, R. (2010). *Albert Camus: Elements of a life.* New York: Cornell University Press.

Zimmerman, B., & Schunk, D. H. (Eds.). (2011). *Handbook of self-regulation of learning and performance.* New York: Routledge.

Index

About the Authors

Carol A. Mullen, PhD, is professor of educational leadership at Virginia Tech, Blacksburg, Virginia, where she is director of the School of Education and associate dean for professional education of the College of Liberal Arts and Human Sciences. She has taught in research-tier universities since 1995 in the United States, and for years prior taught in community college systems in Canada. She is a Kappa Delta Pi representative to the United Nations on behalf of the UN Department of Public Information. Her research interests include mentoring theory and practice, social justice in educational leadership contexts, and applied scholarly writing. Her scholarly roots are in narrative inquiry and educational studies. Her authorships encompass more than two hundred refereed journal articles and book chapters, eighteen special issues of journals, and nineteen books. Recent books are the coauthored book *Shifting to Fit: The Politics of Black and White Identity in School Leadership* (Information Age Publishing, 2014); the coedited volume *The SAGE Handbook of Mentoring and Coaching in Education* (SAGE, 2012); and, as single author, *From Student to Professor: Translating a Graduate Degree into a Career in Academia* (Rowman & Littlefield Education, 2012).

Mullen has published and presented numerous works on arts-based educational research. Her scholarship on the use of visual data in research has appeared in journal article form—specifically on arts-based educational programming for incarcerated women (e.g., *Studies in Art Education,* 1999)—and book form (e.g., *The Postmodern Educator: Arts-Based Inquiries and Teacher Development,* 1999). For the 2012–2013 term Mullen served as the sixty-seventh president of the National Council of Professors of Educational Administration (NCPEA). Her PhD is from the Ontario Institute for Studies in Education of the University of Toronto, Canada.

Fenwick W. English, PhD, is the R. Wendell Eaves Senior Professor of Educational Leadership in the School of Education at the University of North Carolina at Chapel Hill, a position he has held since 2001. He is a former public school elementary and middle school teacher, middle school assistant principal and principal in California, assistant superintendent of schools in Florida, and superintendent of schools in New York. He also served as associate executive director of the AASA and a partner in the consulting and accounting firm of Peat, Marwick & Mitchell in Washington, DC. In academic administration he has been a department chair, dean, and vice-chancellor of academic affairs at universities in Ohio and Indiana. He is the author or coauthor of more than thirty books in education and one hundred-plus journal articles including publications in *Educational Administration Quarterly, Educational Policy, Educational Researcher, International Journal of Leadership in Education, Journal of Educational Administration and History, Journal of Educational Administration, Journal of School Leadership, Leadership and Policy in Schools, Studies in Philosophy and Education,* and *Theory and Practice.* He has published scholarship on the use of visual data in research (*Educational Researcher*, 1988).

With SAGE Publications, he served as the editor of the 2006 SAGE *Encyclopedia of Educational Leadership and Administration* (two volumes); the 2009 SAGE *Library of Educational Thought and Practice: Educational*

Leadership and Administration (four volumes), and the 2011 SAGE *Handbook of Educational Leadership* (2nd ed.). He is the former president of both NCPEA (2011–2012) and the University Council for Educational Administration (UCEA) (2005–2006). He received the NCPEA Living Legend Award in 2013. His PhD is from Arizona State University.

William A. Kealy, PhD, has had a fulfilling career as an associate professor of instructional technology. During his twenty-two-year academic career, he served on the faculty at the University of North Carolina at Greensboro, the University of South Florida (where he was tenured), Florida State University, Texas A&M, and Ithaca College. His research on ways to improve the effectiveness of instructional media has appeared in such journals as *British Journal of Educational Psychology*, *Contemporary Educational Psychology*, *Educational Technology Research and Development*, *Journal of Educational Psychology*, and *Reading Psychology*.

Prior to obtaining his doctorate in learning and instructional technology, Kealy served as art director for a Honolulu-based advertising agency. Within research universities, he taught visual information design and production for twenty-two years. He has a fine arts degree in painting and sculpture and is an accomplished artist. Additionally, he has published numerous empirical studies on learning from the graphic display of information. His PhD is from Arizona State University.